PATISSERIE ERIC

DESSERT
PAIRING
BOOK

CONTENTS

APPLE 사과

FRUIT 과일/열매	
apricot	살구
banana	바나나
blueberry	블루베리
blackberry	블랙베리
black currant	블랙 커런트
cherry	체리
chestnut	밤
cranberry	크랜베리
date	대추
fig	무화과
grape	포도
lemon	레몬
mango	망고
orange	오렌지
pear	배
pineapple	파인애플
plum	자두
pomegranate	석류
quince	모과
raisin	건포도
raspberry	라즈베리
red currant	레드 커런트
lychee	리치
coconut	코코넛

NUT 견과류	
almond	아몬드
cashewnut	캐슈넛
hazelnut	헤이즐넛
walnut	호두
pecan	피칸
peanut	땅콩
pinenut	잣
pistachio	피스타치오

LIQUEUR / WINE 리큐르 / 와인	
armagnac	아르마냑 (프랑스산 브랜디의 일종)
bourbon	버번 (위스키)
brandy	브랜디 (포도 발효 증류술)
calvados	칼바도스 (사과 증류술)
rum	럼

VEGETABLE 채소	
beet	비트
carrot	당근
chili	고추
cucumber	오이
pumpkin	호박
rhubarb	루바브
sweet potato	고구마

SPICE
향신료

allspice	올스파이스 (자메이카 향신료)
black pepper	흑후추
cardamom	카다멈
clove	정향
cinnamon	시나몬
coriander	고수
ginger	생강
fennel	펜넬 (회향)
horseradish	서양 고추냉이
nutmeg	육두구
star anise	팔각
tamarind	타마린드
vanilla	바닐라

HERB
허브

lavender	라벤더
mint	민트
rosemary	로즈마리

GRAIN
곡물

lentil	렌틸콩
oat	오트
rice	쌀

OHTERS
기타

agave nectar	아가베 시럽
apple butter	사과 버터
bacon	베이컨
brown sugar	황설탕
blue cheese	블루 치즈
butter	버터
butterscotch	버터스카치 (스카치 캔디)
buttermilk	버터밀크
caramel	캐러멜
cheddar cheese	체더 치즈
crème fraiche	크렘 프레슈
carbonated soft drink	사이다
custard	커스터드
cream cheese	크림 치즈
camembert cheese	카망베르 치즈
feta cheese	페타 치즈
gorgonzola cheese	고르곤졸라 치즈
granola	그래놀라
white cheese	화이트 치즈
goat cheese	염소 치즈
honey	꿀
maple syrup	메이플 시럽
mascarpone	마스카르포네
molasses	당밀
sour cream	사워 크림

APRICOT 살구

FRUIT 과일/열매	
apple	사과
blueberry	블루베리
cherry	체리
coconut	코코넛
cranberry	크랜베리
fig	무화과
grapefruit	자몽
lemon	레몬
lime	라임
nectarine	천도복숭아
mango	망고
orange	오렌지
peach	복숭아
pineapple	파인애플
plum	자두
raisin	건포도
raspberry	라즈베리
strawberry	딸기

LIQUEUR / WINE 리큐르 / 와인	
brandy	브랜디 (포도 발효 증류술)
cognac	코냑
madeira wine	마데이라 와인 (강화 와인)
muscat wine	뮈스카 와인 (강화 와인)
orange liqueur	오렌지 리큐르
kirsch	키르쉬 (체리 증류술)
rum	럼
wine	와인

HERB 허브	
basil	바질
lemon thyme	레몬 타임
lemongrass	레몬그라스
mint	민트
thyme	타임

NUT 견과류	
almond	아몬드
hazelnut	헤이즐넛
pecan	피칸
pinenut	잣
pistachio	피스타치오
walnut	호두

VEGETABLE 채소	
arugula	루콜라
beet	비트
carrot	당근
cucumber	오이
sweet potato	고구마
pumpkin	호박

SPICE 향신료	
bay leaf	월계수 잎
black pepper	흑후추
cardamom	카다멈
cinnamon	시나몬
clove	정향
coriander	고수
curry	커리
coffee	커피
fennel	펜넬 (회향)
garlic	마늘
ginger	생강
nutmeg	육두구
saffron	사프란
tarragon	타라곤
vanilla	바닐라
white pepper	백후추

GRAIN 곡물	
barley	보리
brown rice	현미
bulgur	불구르 (데친 밀을 말려 빻은 시리얼)
rice	쌀
quinoa	퀴노아
sesame seed	참깨
wheat berry	밀알

OHTERS 기타	
balsamic vinegar	발사믹 식초
brown sugar	황설탕
brie cheese	브리 치즈
butter	버터
buttermilk	버터밀크
caramel	캐러멜
cereal	시리얼
cream	생크림
cream cheese	크림 치즈
cottage cheese	코티지 치즈
chocolate (dark, white)	초콜릿 (다크, 화이트)
goat cheese	염소 치즈
granola	그래놀라
honey	꿀
maple syrup	메이플 시럽
mascarpone	마스카르포네
ricotta cheese	리코타 치즈
sour cream	사워 크림
soft white cheese	소프트 화이트 치즈
white wine vinegar	화이트와인 식초
yogurt	요거트

DRIED APRICOT 건살구

FRUIT 과일/열매	
apple	사과
banana	바나나
chestnut	밤
coconut	코코넛
cranberry	크랜베리
raspberry	라즈베리
dried cherry	건체리
dried currant	건커런트
prune	건자두
raisin	건포도
lemon	레몬
lime	라임
orange	오렌지
pear	배

NUT 견과류	
almond	아몬드
hazelnut	헤이즐넛
pecan	피칸
pinenut	잣
pistachio	피스타치오
walnut	호두

LIQUEUR / WINE 리큐르 / 와인	
brandy	브랜디 (포도 발효 증류술)
cognac	코냑
madeira wine	마데이라 와인 (강화 와인)
muscat wine	뮈스카 와인 (강화 와인)

HERB 허브	
mint	민트
parsley	파슬리

SPICE
향신료

allspice	올스파이스 (자메이카 향신료)
cinnamon	시나몬
curry powder	커리 파우더
ginger	생강
vanilla	바닐라

VEGETABLE
채소

chili	고추
kale	케일
sweet potato	고구마

GRAIN
곡물

bulgur	불구르 (데친 밀을 말려 빻은 시리얼)
rice	쌀
wild rice	야생벼

OHTERS
기타

brown sugar	황설탕
brie cheese	브리 치즈
goat cheese	염소 치즈
ricotta cheese	리코타 치즈
mascarpone	마스카르포네
chocolate (dark, milk, white)	초콜릿 (다크, 밀크, 화이트)
honey	꿀
maple syrup	메이플 시럽
champagne vinegar	샴페인 식초
rice vinegar	쌀 식초

ASIAN PEAR 돌배

FRUIT
과일/열매

apple	사과
blackberry	블랙베리
blueberry	블루베리
fig	무화과
plum	자두
raisin	건포도
raspberry	라즈베리

NUT
견과류

almond	아몬드
cashewnut	캐슈넛
hazelnut	헤이즐넛
macadamia	마카다미아
pistachio	피스타치오
pecan	피칸

LIQUEUR / WINE
리큐르 / 와인

bourbon	버번 (위스키)
brandy	브랜디 (포도 발효 증류술)
rum	럼

SPICE
향신료

allspice	올스파이스 (자메이카 향신료)
black pepper	흑후추
cardamom	카다멈
clove	정향
cinnamon	시나몬
ginger	생강
nutmeg	육두구
vanilla	바닐라

OHTERS
기타

black tea	홍차
brown butter	브라운 버터
butterscotch	버터스카치 (스카치 캔디)
caramel	캐러멜
honey	꿀
maple syrup	메이플 시럽
mascarpone	마스카르포네

NOTE.

BANANA / RED BANANA 바나나 / 레드 바나나

FRUIT 과일/열매	
apple	사과
apricot	살구
blackberry	블랙베리
blueberry	블루베리
cherry	체리
coconut	코코넛
date	대추
fig	무화과
guava	구아바
lemon	레몬
lime	라임
nectarine	천도복숭아
mango	망고
orange	오렌지
papaya	파파야
passion fruit	패션프루트
peach	복숭아
pear	배
pineapple	파인애플
pomegranate	석류
raisin	건포도
raspberry	라즈베리
strawberry	딸기
yuzu	유자

NUT 견과류	
almond	아몬드
brazilnut	브라질너트
cashewnut	캐슈넛
hazelnut	헤이즐넛
macadamia	마카다미아
sunflower seed	해바라기씨
peanut	땅콩
pecan	피칸
pistachio	피스타치오
walnut	호두

LIQUEUR / WINE 리큐르 / 와인	
armagnac	아르마냑 (프랑스산 브랜디의 일종)
bourbon	버번 (위스키)
brandy	브랜디 (포도 발효 증류술)
calvados	칼바도스 (사과 증류술)
cognac	코냑
kirsch	키르쉬 (체리 증류술)
rum	럼

HERB 허브	
lemongrass	레몬그라스

SPICE
향신료

allspice	올스파이스 (자메이카 향신료)
black pepper	흑후추
cardamom	카다멈
cinnamon	시나몬
clove	정향
coffee	커피
coriander	고수
curry	커리
ginger	생강
nutmeg	육두구
tamarind	타마린드
vanilla	바닐라

VEGETABLE
채소

beet	비트
chili	고추
sweet potato	고구마
pumpkin	호박

GRAIN
곡물

baked bean	구운 콩
black sesame	검은깨
flax seed	아마씨
oat	오트
sesame seed	참깨
quinoa	퀴노아

OHTERS
기타

agave nectar	아가베 시럽
brown butter	브라운 버터
brown sugar	황설탕
buttermilk	버터밀크
butterscotch	버터스카치 (스카치 캔디)
caramel	캐러멜
cereals	시리얼
chocolate (dark, milk, white)	초콜릿 (다크, 밀크, 화이트)
cream cheese	크림 치즈
crème fraiche	크렘 프레슈
honey	꿀
maple syrup	메이플 시럽
molasses	당밀
ricotta cheese	리코타 치즈
sour cream	사워 크림

PLANTAIN 플랜테인 (바나나의 일종)

FRUIT
과일/열매

coconut	코코넛
cranberry	크랜베리
lemon	레몬
lime	라임
orange	오렌지
pineapple	파인애플

SPICE
향신료

all spice	올스파이스 (자메이카 향신료)
black pepper	흑후추
cinnamon	시나몬
ginger	생강
star anise	팔각

NUT
견과류

almond	아몬드

OHTERS
기타

cheese	치즈
dark chocolate	다크초콜릿
coconut oil	코코넛오일
honey	꿀
olive oil	올리브오일

LIQUEUR / WINE
리큐르 / 와인

rum	럼
madeira wine	마데이라 와인 (강화 와인)

NOTE.

BLOOD ORANGE 블러드 오렌지

FRUIT 과일/열매	
avocado	아보카도
fig	무화과
grapefruit	자몽
kiwi	키위
kumquat	금귤
lemon	레몬
lime	라임
mango	망고
orange	오렌지
papaya	파파야
pomegranate	석류
olive	올리브
tangerine	귤

HERB 허브	
mint	민트
thyme	타임

SPICE 향신료	
allspice	올스파이스 (자메이카 향신료)
cardamom	카다멈
cinnamon	시나몬
clove	정향
coriander	고수
fennel	펜넬 (회향)
ginger	생강
vanilla	바닐라

NUT 견과류	
almond	아몬드
pistachio	피스타치오
walnut	호두

VEGETABLE 채소	
arugula	루콜라
beet	비트
chili	고추
watercress	물냉이
spinach	시금치

LIQUEUR / WINE 리큐르 / 와인	
wine	와인
champagne	샴페인

GRAIN 곡물	
quinoa	퀴노아

OHTERS 기타	
blue cheese	블루 치즈
brown sugar	황설탕
caramel	캐러멜
chocolate (dark, white)	초콜릿 (다크, 화이트)
feta cheese	페타 치즈
goat cheese	염소 치즈
honey	꿀
balsamic vinegar	발사믹 식초
white wine vinegar	화이트와인 식초

BLUEBERRY 블루베리

FRUIT
과일/열매

apple	사과
apricot	살구
banana	바나나
blackberry	블랙베리
current	커런트
mango	망고
grapefruit	자몽
lemon	레몬
lime	라임
melon	멜론
nectarine	천도복숭아
orange	오렌지
peach	복숭아
pear	배
pineapple	파인애플
raspberry	라즈베리
strawberry	딸기
watermelon	수박

NUT
견과류

almond	아몬드
hazelnut	헤이즐넛
pecan	피칸
pinenut	잣
walnut	호두

LIQUEUR / WINE
리큐르 / 와인

brandy	브랜디 (포도 발효 증류술)
rum	럼

HERB
허브

lavender	라벤더
mint	민트
thyme	타임

SPICE
향신료

allspice	올스파이스 (자메이카 향신료)
black pepper	흑후추
cinnamon	시나몬
clove	정향
ginger	생강
nutmeg	육두구
vanilla	바닐라

VEGETABLE
채소

cucumber	오이
rhubarb	루바브

GRAIN 곡물	
brown rice	현미
corn	옥수수

OHTERS 기타	
agave nectar	아가베 시럽
buttermilk	버터밀크
blue cheese	블루 치즈
cereal	시리얼
cream	생크림
cream cheese	크림 치즈
crème fraiche	크렘 프레슈
granola	그래놀라
honey	꿀
maple syrup	메이플 시럽
mascarpone	마스카르포네
molasses	당밀
ricotta cheese	리코타 치즈
sour cream	샤워 크림
white chocolate	화이트초콜릿
yogurt	요거트

CHERRY 체리

FRUIT 과일/열매	
apple	사과
apricot	살구
blackberry	블랙배리
fig	무화과
lemon	레몬
lime	라임
nectarine	천도복숭아
melon	멜론
orange	오렌지
pear	배
peach	복숭아
plum	자두
quince	모과
red current	레드 커런트
raspberry	라즈베리

NUT 견과류	
almond	아몬드
hazelnut	헤이즐넛
pecan	피칸
pistachio	피스타치오
walnut	호두

LIQUEUR / WINE 리큐르 / 와인	
armagnac	아르마냑 (프랑스산 브랜디의 일종)
brandy	브랜디 (포도 발효 증류술)
dry wine	드라이 와인
kirsch	키르쉬 (체리 증류술)
red wine	레드와인
rum	럼

HERB 허브	
basil	바질
lemon verbena	레몬 버베나
mint	민트

SPICE 향신료	
allspice	올스파이스 (자메이카 향신료)
black pepper	흑후추
cardamom	카다멈
cinnamon	시나몬
coffee	커피
nutmeg	육두구
star anise	팔각
vanilla	바닐라

VEGETABLE
채소

rhubarb	루바브

GRAIN
곡물

oat	오트

OHTERS
기타

balsamic vinegar	발사믹 식초
butter	버터
buttermilk	버터밀크
caramel	캐러멜
chocolate (dark, milk, white)	초콜릿 (다크, 밀크, 화이트)
cream cheese	크림 치즈
crème fraiche	크렘 프레슈
cream	생크림
goat cheese	염소 치즈
honey	꿀
mascarpone	마스카르포네
olive oil	올리브오일
peanut butter	땅콩 버터
ricotta cheese	리코타 치즈
sour cream	사워 크림
yogurt	요거트

CHESTNUT 밤

FRUIT
과일/열매

apple	사과
fig	무화과
grape	포도
lemon	레몬
pear	배
prune	건자두
orange	오렌지
raisin	건포도
raspberry	라즈베리

NUT
견과류

pecan	피칸
pinenut	잣

LIQUEUR / WINE
리큐르 / 와인

armagnac	아르마냑 (프랑스산 브랜디의 일종)
brandy	브랜디 (포도 발효 증류술)
cognac	코냑
marsala	마르살라 와인 (강화 와인)
rum	럼

HERB
허브

parsley	파슬리
rosemary	로즈마리

SPICE
향신료

bay leaf	월계수 잎
black pepper	흑후추
cardamom	카다멈
cinnamon	시나몬
clove	정향
coffee	커피
fennel	펜넬 (회향)
garlic	마늘
ginger	생강
chipotle chili	치폴레 칠리 (멕시코산 고추를 구워 건조한 것)
nutmeg	육두구
tarragon	타라곤
vanilla	바닐라

VEGETABLE
채소

beet	비트
carrot	당근
kale	케일
parsnip	파스닙
pumpkin	호박

GRAIN
곡물

chickpea	병아리콩
farro	파로
glutinous rice	찹쌀
lentil	렌틸콩

OHTERS
기타

balsamic vinegar	발사믹 식초
blue cheese	블루 치즈
brown sugar	황설탕
button mushroom	양송이버섯
canola oil	카놀라오일
caramel	캐러멜
chocolate (dark, milk, white)	초콜릿 (다크, 밀크, 화이트)
crème fraiche	크렘 프레슈
fontina cheese	폰티나 치즈
grape seed oil	포도씨오일
honey	꿀
maple syrup	메이플 시럽
mascarpone	마스카르포네
milk	우유
olive oil	올리브오일
red wine vinegar	레드와인 식초
ricotta cheese	리코타 치즈
sea salt	바닷소금
sesame seed oil	참기름
sherry wine vinegar	셰리 와인 식초

COCONUT 코코넛

FRUIT 과일/열매	
apple	사과
apricot	살구
avocado	아보카도
banana	바나나
blackberry	블랙베리
cherry	체리
date	대추
fig	무화과
grapefruit	자몽
goji berry	구기자 열매
kumquat	금귤
kiwi	키위
lemon	레몬
lime	라임
lychee	리치
mango	망고
melon	멜론
orange	오렌지
papaya	파파야
passion fruit	패션프루트
pineapple	파인애플
pomegranate	석류
plantain	플렌틴 (바나나의 일종)
raspberry	라즈베리
strawberry	딸기

NUT 견과류	
almond	아몬드
cashewnut	캐슈넛
macadamia	마카다미아
pecan	피칸
pistachio	피스타치오

LIQUEUR / WINE 리큐르 / 와인	
rum	럼

HERB 허브	
lemongrass	레몬그라스
basil	바질
mint	민트

SPICE
향신료

allspice	올스파이스 (자메이카 향신료)
coriander	고수
curry	커리
cinnamon	시나몬
garlic	마늘
ginger	생강
pepper	후추
nutmeg	육두구
vanilla	바닐라

VEGETABLE
채소

carrot	당근
chili	고추
cucumber	오이
paprika	파프리카
pumpkin	호박
spinach	시금치

GRAIN
곡물

oat	오트
sesame seed	참깨
chia seed	치아씨드
lentil	렌틸콩

OHTERS
기타

bacon	베이컨
cereal	시리얼
mascarpone	마스카르포네
maple syrup	메이플 시럽
honey	꿀
chocolate (white, milk, dark)	초콜릿 (화이트, 밀크, 다크)
caramel	캐러멜
cheese	치즈
coconut milk	코코넛 밀크
coconut butter	코코넛 버터
green tea	녹차
peanut butter	땅콩 버터
milk	우유
miso	미소 (일본식 된장)
soy sauce	간장
butterscotch syrup	스카치 캔디 시럽
tapioca	타피오카
vinegar	식초
yogurt	요거트

CRANBERRY 크랜베리

FRUIT
과일/열매

apple	사과
apricot	살구
lemon	레몬
lime	라임
orange	오렌지
peach	복숭아
pear	배
raisin	건포도
quince	모과
tangerine	귤
persimmon	단감
pomegranate	석류
watermelon	수박

LIQUEUR / WINE
리큐르 / 와인

port wine	포트 와인
vodka	보드카

SPICE
향신료

allspice	올스파이스 (자메이카 향신료)
cinnamon	시나몬
clove	정향
ginger	생강
nutmeg	육두구
star anise	팔각
vanilla	바닐라

NUT
견과류

almond	아몬드
hazelnut	헤이즐넛
pecan	피칸
pistachio	피스타치오
walnut	호두

VEGETABLE
채소

beet	비트
pumpkin	호박
spinach	시금치

OHTERS 기타	
brown sugar	황설탕
cream cheese	크림 치즈
goat cheese	염소 치즈
granola	그래놀라
soft cheese	소프트 치즈
honey	꿀
maple syrup	메이플 시럽
popcorn	팝콘
chocolate (dark, milk, white)	초콜릿 (다크, 밀크, 화이트)
yogurt	요거트

 **FIG** 무화과

FRUIT
과일/열매

apple	사과
banana	바나나
chestnut	밤
coconut	코코넛
cranberry	크랜베리
date	대추
grape	포도
lemon	레몬
lime	라임
melon	멜론
orange	오렌지
peach	복숭아
pear	배
persimmons	감
pomegranate	석류
quince	모과
raisin	건포도
raspberry	라즈베리
olive	올리브
strawberry	딸기

NUT
견과류

almond	아몬드
hazelnut	헤이즐넛
pistachio	피스타치오
pecan	피칸
walnut	호두

LIQUEUR / WINE
리큐르 / 와인

armagnac	아르마냑 (프랑스산 브랜디의 일종)
brandy	브랜디 (포도 발효 증류술)
cointreau	쿠앵트로 (오렌지 증류술)
port wine	포트 와인
red wine	레드와인
sweet wine	스위트 와인

HERB
허브

basil	바질
lavender	라벤더
mint	민트
rosemary	로즈마리
thyme	타임

SPICE
향신료

anise	아니스
bay leaf	월계수 잎
cardamom	카다멈
clove	정향
cinnamon	시나몬
black pepper	흑후추
fennel	펜넬 (회향)
ginger	생강
star anise	팔각
vanilla	바닐라

VEGETABLE 채소	
spinach	시금치
pumpkin	호박

GRAIN 곡물	
sesame seed	참깨

OHTERS 기타	
butter	버터
caramel	캐러멜
cereal	시리얼
granola	그래놀라
blue cheese	블루 치즈
burrata cheese	부라타 치즈
cabrales cheese	카브랄레스 치즈
chevre cheese	염소젖 치즈
cream cheese	크림 치즈
feta cheese	페타 치즈
fresh white cheese	프레시 화이트 치즈
goat cheese	염소 치즈
gorgonzola cheese	고르곤졸라 치즈
Manchego cheese	만체고 치즈
monterey jack cheese	몬테레이 잭 치즈
mozzarella cheese	모차렐라 치즈
parmesan cheese	파르메산 치즈

pecorino cheese	페코리노 치즈
ricotta cheese	리코타 치즈
stilton cheese	스틸턴 치즈
chocolate (dark, milk, white)	초콜릿 (다크, 밀크, 화이트)
crème fraiche	크렘 프레슈
honey	꿀
mascarpone	마스카르포네
milk	우유
oil	식용유
sour cream	사워 크림
balsamic vinegar	발사믹 식초
red wine vinegar	레드와인 식초
sherry vinegar	셰리주 식초
white balsamic vinegar	화이트 발사믹 식초
yogurt	요거트

GRAPE 포도

FRUIT
과일/열매

apple	사과
banana	바나나
blueberry	블루베리
fig	무화과
grapefruit	자몽
lemon	레몬
lime	라임
mango	망고
melon	멜론
orange	오렌지
pear	배
raspberry	라즈베리
strawberry	딸기
watermelon	수박
coconut	코코넛

NUT
견과류

almond	아몬드
hazelnut	헤이즐넛
peanut	땅콩
pecan	피칸
pistachio	피스타치오
walnut	호두

LIQUEUR / WINE
리큐르 / 와인

rum	럼

HERB
허브

basil	바질
mint	민트
rosemary	로즈마리
parsley	파슬리

SPICE
향신료

cinnamon	시나몬
clove	정향
fennel	펜넬 (회향)
garlic	마늘
ginger	생강
nutmeg	육두구
star anise	팔각

VEGETABLE
채소

carrot	당근
celery	샐러리
chili	고추
cucumber	오이
watercress	물냉이
tomato	토마토

GRAIN
곡물

bulgur	불구르 (데친 밀을 말려 빻은 시리얼)
brown rice	현미
quinoa	퀴노아

OHTERS
기타

agave nectar	아가베 시럽
apple butter	사과 버터
bacon	베이컨
brown sugar	황설탕
blue cheese	블루 치즈
butter	버터
butterscotch	버터스카치 (스카치 캔디)
buttermilk	버터밀크
caramel	캐러멜
cheddar cheese	체더 치즈
crème fraiche	크렘 프레슈
carbonated soft drink	사이다
custard	커스터드
cream cheese	크림 치즈
camembert cheese	카망베르 치즈
feta cheese	페타 치즈
gorgonzola cheese	고르곤졸라 치즈
white cheese	화이트 치즈
goat cheese	염소 치즈
granola	그래놀라
honey	꿀
maple syrup	메이플 시럽
mascarpone	마스카르포네
molasses	당밀
sour cream	사워 크림

GRAPEFRUIT 자몽

FRUIT
과일/열매

avocado	아보카도
banana	바나나
coconut	코코넛
kiwi	키위
lemon	레몬
melon	멜론
orange	오렌지
papaya	파파야
pear	배
pineapple	파인애플
pomegranate	석류
raspberry	라즈베리
olive	올리브
strawberry	딸기

NUT
견과류

cashewnut	캐슈넛
hazelnut	헤이즐넛
macadamia	마카다미아
pecan	피칸
pistachio	피스타치오
walnut	호두

LIQUEUR / WINE
리큐르 / 와인

campari	캄파리 (이탈리아 술)
mirin	미림 (맛술)
rum	럼
sparkling wine	스파클링 와인
port wine	포트 와인
vodka	보드카

HERB
허브

mint	민트
parsley	파슬리

SPICE
향신료

cinnamon	시나몬
coriander	고수
fennel	펜넬 (회향)
ginger	생강
star anise	팔각
tarragon	타라곤
vanilla	바닐라

VEGETABLE 채소	
beet	비트
chili	고추

OHTERS 기타	
agave syrup	아가베 시럽
brown sugar	황설탕
caramel	캐러멜
fromage blanc cheese	프로마주 블랑 치즈
feta cheese	페타 치즈
parmesan cheese	파르메산 치즈
honey	꿀
maple syrup	메이플 시럽
olive oil	올리브오일
yogurt	요거트
champagne vinegar	샴페인 식초
rice vinegar	쌀 식초
wine vinegar	와인 식초
sherry vinegar	셰리주 식초
white wine vinegar	화이트와인 식초

KIWI 키위

FRUIT 과일/열매	
apple	사과
banana	바나나
blood orange	블러드 오렌지
cherry	체리
coconut	코코넛
grape	포도
grapefruit	자몽
honeydew melon	허니듀 멜론
lemon	레몬
lime	라임
lychee	리치
mango	망고
melon	멜론
orange	오렌지
passion fruit	패션프루트
papaya	파파야
pineapple	파인애플
pomegranate	석류
raspberry	라즈베리
star fruit	스타 프루트
strawberry	딸기
watermelon	수박

NUT 견과류	
almond	아몬드
cashewnut	캐슈넛
hazelnut	헤이즐넛
macadamia	마카다미아
pistachio	피스타치오

LIQUEUR / WINE 리큐르 / 와인	
cointreau	쿠앵트로 (오렌지 증류술)
ice wine	아이스 와인
kirsch	키르쉬 (체리 증류술)
sweet champagne	스위트 샴페인
rum	럼

HERB 허브	
mint	민트

SPICE 향신료	
cinnamon	시나몬
ginger	생강
vanilla	바닐라

VEGETABLE 채소	
cucumber	오이

OHTERS 기타	
brown sugar	황설탕
cereal	시리얼
chocolate (dark, milk, white)	초콜릿 (다크, 밀크, 화이트)
honey	꿀
yogurt	요거트

KUMQUAT 금귤

FRUIT 과일/열매	
apple	사과
apricot	살구
avocado	아보카도
banana	바나나
blackberry	블랙베리
cherry	체리
date	대추
fig	무화과
grapefruit	자몽
green apple	청사과
lemon	레몬
lime	라임
mango	망고
orange	오렌지
papaya	파파야
persimmon	감
pineapple	파인애플
plum	자두
raisin	건포도
raspberry	라즈베리
star fruit	스타 프루트
strawberry	딸기

NUT 견과류	
pistachio	피스타치오
walnut	호두

LIQUEUR / WINE 리큐르 / 와인	
brandy	브랜디 (포도 발효 증류술)
rum	럼

HERB 허브	
mint	민트

SPICE 향신료	
anise	아니스
cinnamon	시나몬
clove	정향
coffee	커피
coriander	고수
ginger	생강
pink peppercorn	핑크페퍼
vanilla	바닐라

VEGETABLE
채소

beet	비트
rhubarb	루바브

GRAIN
곡물

bulgur	불구르 (데친 밀을 말려 빻은 시리얼)

OHTERS
기타

brown sugar	황설탕
chili powder	고춧가루
chocolate (dark, milk, white)	초콜릿 (다크, 밀크, 화이트)
buttermilk	버터밀크
honey	꿀
shiitake mushroom	표고버섯
wine vinegar	와인 식초

LEMON 레몬

FRUIT 과일/열매	
apple	사과
apricot	살구
avocado	아보카도
banana	바나나
blackberry	블랙베리
blueberry	블루베리
cherry	체리
chestnut	밤
coconut	코코넛
cranberry	크랜베리
date	대추
fig	무화과
grapefruit	자몽
grape	포도
gooseberry	구스베리
guava	구아바
kiwi	키위
lime	라임
mango	망고
nectarine	천도복숭아
orange	오렌지
papaya	파파야
passion fruit	패션프루트
peach	복숭아
pear	배
persimmon	감
plantain	플랜테인 (바나나의 일종)
plum	자두
pricky pear	백년초
prune	건자두
quince	모과

raspberry	라즈베리
strawberry	딸기

NUT 견과류	
almond	아몬드
hazelnut	헤이즐넛
pecan	피칸
pinenut	잣
pistachio	피스타치오

HERB 허브	
basil	바질
dill	딜
lemongrass	레몬그라스
mint	민트
lavender	라벤더
thyme	타임

GRAIN 곡물	
chickpea	병아리콩
corn	옥수수
fava bean	누에콩
green bean	깍지콩
lentil	렌틸콩
pea	완두콩

SPICE
향신료

black pepper	흑후추
cardamom	카다멈
cinnamon	시나몬
coriander	고수
ginger	생강
fennel	펜넬 (회향)
garlic	마늘
coffee	커피
saffron	사프란
vanilla	바닐라
wasabi	와사비
za'atar	자타르 (중동의 혼합 향신료)

VEGETABLE
채소

amaranth	아마란스
artichoke	아티초크
beet	비트
bell pepper	피망
chive	쪽파
cucumber	오이
edamame	풋콩
paprika	파프리카
parsnip	파스닙
rhubarb	루바브
tomato	토마토

LIQUEUR / WINE
리큐르 / 와인

dry white wine	드라이 화이트와인
rum	럼

OHTERS
기타

buttermilk	버터밀크
brown sugar	황설탕
caramel	캐러멜
chocolate (dark, milk, white)	초콜릿 (다크, 밀크, 화이트)
cream cheese	크림 치즈
goat cheese	염소 치즈
pecorino cheese	페코리노 치즈
ricotta cheese	리코타 치즈
honey	꿀
mascarpone	마스카르포네
maple syrup	메이플 시럽
miso	미소 (일본식 된장)
mushroom	버섯
olive oil	올리브오일
sour cream	사워 크림
yogurt	요거트
champagne vinegar	샴페인 식초
rice vinegar	쌀 식초
sherry vinegar	셰리주 식초
wine vinegar	와인 식초

LIME 라임

FRUIT 과일/열매	
apple	사과
apricot	살구
banana	바나나
blackberry	블랙베리
blueberry	블루베리
coconut	코코넛
date	대추
fig	무화과
grapefruit	자몽
guava	구아바
kiwi	키위
lemon	레몬
lychee	리치
mango	망고
melon	멜론
honeydew melon	허니듀 멜론
orange	오렌지
papaya	파파야
pear	배
pomegranate	석류
plum	자두
raspberry	라즈베리
strawberry	딸기
watermelon	수박

NUT 견과류	
almond	아몬드
macadamia	마카다미아
pecan	피칸
hazelnut	헤이즐넛

LIQUEUR / WINE 리큐르 / 와인	
rum	럼
tequila	데킬라

HERB 허브	
basil	바질
lemongrass	레몬그라스
mint	민트
rosemary	로즈마리

SPICE 향신료	
coriander	고수
garlic	마늘
ginger	생강
tarragon	타라곤
vanilla	바닐라

VEGETABLE
채소

carrot	당근
chili	고추
tomato	토마토

GRAIN
곡물

corn	옥수수
quinoa	퀴노아
sesame seed	참깨

OHTERS
기타

buttermilk	버터밀크
brown sugar	황설탕
caramel	캐러멜
cream cheese	크림치즈
cotija cheese	코티하 치즈
green tea	녹차
honey	꿀
mascarpone	마스카르포네
mushroom	버섯
grape seed oil	포도씨오일
olive oil	올리브오일
sunflower seed oil	해바라기씨오일
sesame seed oil	참기름
soy sauce	간장
tapioca	타피오카
champagne vinegar	샴페인 식초
rice vinegar	쌀 식초
sherry vinegar	셰리주 식초
white chocolate	화이트초콜릿
yogurt	요거트

LYCHEE 리치

FRUIT 과일/열매	
blackberry	블랙베리
blueberry	블루베리
cherry	체리
coconut	코코넛
grapefruit	자몽
kiwi	키위
lemon	레몬
lime	라임
mango	망고
melon	멜론
honeydew melon	허니듀 멜론
nectarine	천도복숭아
orange	오렌지
passion fruit	패션프루트
peach	복숭아
pear	배
pineapple	파인애플
plum	자두
raspberry	라즈베리
strawberry	딸기

NUT 견과류	
almond	아몬드

VEGETABLE 채소	
chili	고추

LIQUEUR / WINE 리큐르 / 와인	
rum	럼
gin	진
plum wine	매실주
sparkling wine	스파클링 와인
vodka	보드카

HERB 허브	
lemongrass	레몬그라스
mint	민트

SPICE 향신료	
coriander	고수
garlic	마늘
ginger	생강
vanilla	바닐라

OHTERS 기타	
brown sugar	황설탕
palm sugar	야자 설탕
cream cheese	크림 치즈
chocolate (dark, milk, white)	초콜릿 (다크, 밀크, 화이트)
honey	꿀
rose water	장미수
yogurt	요거트

NOTE.

MANGO 망고

FRUIT 과일/열매	
apple	사과
avocado	아보카도
banana	바나나
blackberry	블랙베리
blueberry	블루베리
coconut	코코넛
grapefruit	자몽
kiwi	키위
kumquat	금귤
lemon	레몬
lime	라임
melon	멜론
nectarine	천도복숭아
orange	오렌지
papaya	파파야
passion fruit	패션프루트
peaches	복숭아
pear	배
pineapple	파인애플
raspberry	라즈베리
strawberry	딸기

LIQUEUR / WINE 리큐르 / 와인	
kirsch	키르쉬 (체리 증류술)
rum	럼

HERB 허브	
basil	바질
mint	민트
oregano	오레가노
parsley	파슬리
lavender	라벤더

SPICE 향신료	
anise	아니스
cayenne	카이엔
cinnamon	시나몬
clove	정향
coffee	커피
coriander	고수
curry	커리
fennel	펜넬 (회향)
garlic	마늘
star anise	팔각
vanilla	바닐라

NUT 견과류	
almond	아몬드
cashewnut	캐슈넛
macadamia	마카다미아
peanut	땅콩

VEGETABLE
채소

bell pepper	피망
cucumber	오이
paprika	파프리카
rhubarb	루바브
spinach	시금치

GRAIN
곡물

cannellini beans	카넬리니콩
chickpea	병아리콩
corn	옥수수
quinoa	퀴노아
sesame seed	참깨

OHTERS
기타

almond milk	아몬드 우유
caramel	캐러멜
dark chocolate	다크초콜릿
honey	꿀
mascarpone	마스카르포네
yogurt	요거트

NECTARINE 천도복숭아

FRUIT
과일/열매

blackberry	블랙베리
blueberry	블루베리
cherry	체리
fig	무화과
lemon	레몬
mango	망고
orange	오렌지
peach	복숭아
plum	자두
raspberry	라즈베리
strawberry	딸기

NUT
견과류

almond	아몬드
hazelnut	헤이즐넛
macadamia	마카다미아

LIQUEUR / WINE
리큐르 / 와인

champagne	샴페인
red wine	레드와인
white wine	화이트와인
still wine	발포성 포도주
sparkling wine	스파클링 와인

HERB
허브

basil	바질
mint	민트
rosemary	로즈마리

SPICE
향신료

black pepper	흑후추
cinnamon	시나몬
ginger	생강
nutmeg	육두구
tarragon	타라곤
vanilla	바닐라

GRAIN
곡물

oat	오트

OHTERS 기타	
buttermilk	버터밀크
blue cheese	블루 치즈
caramel	캐러멜
mozzarella cheese	모차렐라 치즈
honey	꿀
maple syrup	메이플 시럽
mascarpone	마스카르포네
olive oil	올리브오일
balsamic vinegar	발사믹 식초
yogurt	요거트

ORANGE 오렌지

FRUIT 과일/열매	
apple	사과
apricot	살구
avocado	아보카도
banana	바나나
blood orange	블러드 오렌지
blueberry	블루베리
cherry	체리
coconut	코코넛
cranberry	크랜베리
date	대추
fig	무화과
grape	포도
grapefruit	자몽
kiwi	키위
kumquat	금귤
lemon	레몬
lime	라임
mango	망고
melon	멜론
nectarine	천도복숭아
orange	오렌지
papaya	파파야
passion fruit	패션프루트
peach	복숭아
pear	배
pineapple	파인애플
plum	자두
pomegranate	석류
raspberry	라즈베리
star fruit	스타 프루트
black olive	블랙 올리브
kalamata olive	칼라마타 올리브
strawberry	딸기

NUT 견과류	
almond	아몬드
hazelnut	헤이즐넛
macadamia	마카다미아
pecan	피칸
peanut	땅콩
pinenut	잣
pistachio	피스타치오
walnut	호두

LIQUEUR / WINE 리큐르 / 와인	
armagnac	아르마냑 (프랑스산 브랜디의 일종)
cointreau	쿠앵트로 (오렌지 증류술)
grand marnier	그랑 마르니에 (오렌지 큐라소)
red wine	레드와인

HERB
허브

basil	바질
parsley	파슬리
rosemary	로즈마리

SPICE
향신료

allspice	올스파이스 (자메이카 향신료)
anise	아니스
black pepper	흑후추
cardamom	카다멈
cinnamon	시나몬
coffee	커피
coriander	고수
fennel	펜넬 (회향)
garlic	마늘
ginger	생강
vanilla	바닐라

VEGETABLE
채소

beet	비트
carrot	당근
chili	고추
pumpkin	호박
rhubarb	루바브
sweet potato	고구마
yam	마

GRAIN
곡물

black bean	검은콩
chickpea	병아리콩
millet	수수
quinoa	퀴노아

OHTERS
기타

apple cider vinegar	사과 식초
balsamic vinegar	발사믹 식초
champagne vinegar	샴페인 식초
chocolate (dark, white)	초콜릿 (다크, 화이트)
cream cheese	크림 치즈
feta cheese	페타 치즈
goat cheese	염소 치즈
honey	꿀
olive oil	올리브오일
red wine vinegar	레드와인 식초
rice wine vinegar	막걸리 식초
sesame seed oil	참기름
sherry vinegar	셰리주 식초
soy sauce	간장
sunflower seed oil	해바라기씨오일
white wine vinegar	화이트와인 식초

PASSION FRUIT 패션프루트

FRUIT 과일/열매	
apple	사과
banana	바나나
cantaloupe melon	캔털루프 멜론
coconut	코코넛
kiwi	키위
lemon	레몬
lime	라임
mango	망고
orange	오렌지
papaya	파파야
peach	복숭아
pear	배
pineapple	파인애플
plum	자두
raspberry	라즈베리
strawberry	딸기

LIQUEUR / WINE 리큐르 / 와인	
champagne	샴페인
sparkling wine	스파클링 와인
rum	럼
tequila	데킬라
white wine	화이트와인

HERB 허브	
basil	바질
mint	민트
lemongrass	레몬그라스

SPICE 향신료	
cinnamon	시나몬
ginger	생강
vanilla	바닐라

NUT 견과류	
almond	아몬드
cashewnut	캐슈넛
hazelnut	헤이즐넛
macadamia	마카다미아
peanut	땅콩
pistachio	피스타치오

OHTERS 기타	
caramel	캐러멜
white chocokate	화이트초콜릿
cream cheese	크림 치즈
honey	꿀
yogurt	요거트

NOTE.

PEACH 복숭아

FRUIT 과일/열매	
apple	사과
apricot	살구
blackberry	블랙베리
black currant	블랙 커런트
blueberry	블루베리
cherry	체리
coconut	코코넛
fig	무화과
grape	포도
lemon	레몬
lime	라임
lychee	리치
mango	망고
nectarine	천도복숭아
orange	오렌지
papaya	파파야
passion fruit	패션프루트
pineapple	파인애플
plum	자두
pomegranate	석류
raspberry	라즈베리
red currant	레드 커런트
strawberry	딸기
olive	올리브
yuzu	유자

NUT 견과류	
almond	아몬드
cashewnut	캐슈넛
hazelnut	헤이즐넛
macadamia	마카다미아
pecan	피칸
pistachio	피스타치오
walnut	호두

LIQUEUR / WINE 리큐르 / 와인	
bourbon	버번 (위스키)
brandy	브랜디 (포도 발효 증류술)
champagne	샴페인
cognac	코냑
cointreau	쿠앵트로 (오렌지 증류술)
kirsch	키르쉬 (체리 증류술)
prosecco	프로세코 (이탈리아 스파클링 와인)
red wine	레드와인
rum	럼
sauternes	소테른 (프랑스 화이트와인)
sparkling wine	스파클링 와인
white wine	화이트와인

HERB
허브

basil	바질
mint	민트
rosemary	로즈마리
lavender	라벤더
lemongrass	레몬그라스
lemon verbena	레몬 버베나

SPICE
향신료

allspice	올스파이스 (자메이카 향신료)
black pepper	흑후추
cardamom	카다멈
cinnamon	시나몬
clove	정향
coriander	고수
fennel	펜넬 (회향)
ginger	생강
nutmeg	육두구
saffron	사프란
tarragon	타라곤
vanilla	바닐라

VEGETABLE
채소

arugula	루콜라

GRAIN
곡물

oat	오트

OHTERS
기타

apple cider vinegar	사과 식초
balsamic vinegar	발사믹 식초
black tea	홍차
blue cheese	블루 치즈
burrata cheese	부라타 치즈
buttermilk	버터밀크
caramel	캐러멜
chocolate (dark, milk, white)	초콜릿 (다크, 밀크, 화이트)
cream cheese	크림 치즈
crème fraiche	크렘 프레슈
goat cheese	염소 치즈
green tea	녹차
maple syrup	메이플 시럽
mascarpone	마스카르포네
mozzarella cheese	모차렐라 치즈
oil	식용유
rice wine vinegar	막걸리 식초
ricotta cheese	리코타 치즈

PEAR 배

FRUIT
과일/열매

apple	사과
banana	바나나
blackberry	블랙베리
black currant	블랙 커런트
blueberry	블루베리
cherry	체리
chestnut	밤
cranberry	크랜베리
date	대추
fig	무화과
grapefruit	자몽
lemon	레몬
lime	라임
orange	오렌지
passion fruit	패션프루트
persimmon	감
pineapple	파인애플
plum	자두
prune	건자두
quince	모과
raisin	건포도
raspberry	라즈베리
strawberry	딸기

NUT
견과류

almond	아몬드
hazelnut	헤이즐넛
pecan	피칸
pinenut	잣
pistachio	피스타치오
walnut	호두

LIQUEUR / WINE
리큐르 / 와인

bourbon	버번 (위스키)
brandy	브랜디 (포도 발효 증류술)
crème de cassis	크렘 드 카시스 (리큐어)
port wine	포트 와인
red wine	레드와인
rum	럼
white wine	화이트와인

HERB
허브

thyme	타임
mint	민트
rosemary	로즈마리

VEGETABLE
채소

rhubarb	루바브

SPICE
향신료

allspice	올스파이스 (자메이카 향신료)
anise	아니스
black pepper	흑후추
cardamom	카다멈
cinnamon	시나몬
clove	정향
fennel	펜넬 (회향)
ginger	생강
nutmeg	육두구
star anise	팔각
tarragon	타라곤
vanilla	바닐라

GRAIN
곡물

oat	오트

OHTERS
기타

agave syrup	아가베 시럽
apple cider vinegar	사과 식초
balsamic vinegar	발사믹 식초
blue cheese	블루 치즈
brie cheese	브리 치즈
caramel	캐러멜

chocolate (dark, milk, white)	초콜릿 (다크, 밀크, 화이트)
cream cheese	크림 치즈
feta cheese	페타 치즈
fruit vinegar	과일 식초
goat cheese	염소 치즈
gorgonzola cheese	고르곤졸라 치즈
gruyere cheese	그뤼에르 치즈
grape seed oil	포도씨오일
halloumi cheese	할루미 치즈
honey	꿀
maple syrup	메이플 시럽
olive oil	올리브오일
parmesan cheese	파르메산 치즈
pecorino cheese	페코리노 치즈
raspberry vinegar	라즈베리 식초
red oil	레드 오일
rice vinegar	쌀 식초
ricotta cheese	리코타 치즈
roquefort cheese	로크포르 치즈
sherry vinegar	셰리주 식초
sour cream	사워 크림
stilton cheese	스틸톤 치즈
white vinegar	화이트 식초

PERSIMMON 감

FRUIT
과일/열매

apple	사과
avocado	아보카도
banana	바나나
cherry	체리
cranberry	크랜베리
fig	무화과
grapefruit	자몽
red grape	적포도
kiwi	키위
kumquat	금귤
lemon	레몬
lime	라임
orange	오렌지
pear	배
pineapple	파인애플
pomegranate	석류
raisin	건포도
yuzu	유자

NUT
견과류

almond	아몬드
hazelnut	헤이즐넛
pecan	피칸

LIQUEUR / WINE
리큐르 / 와인

bourbon	버번 (위스키)
brandy	브랜디 (포도 발효 증류술)

SPICE
향신료

black pepper	흑후추
cinnamon	시나몬
ginger	생강
nutmeg	육두구
vanilla	바닐라

VEGETABLE
채소

sweet tomato	고구마
yam	마

GRAIN
곡물

barley	보리
sesame seed	참깨

OHTERS 기타	
agave nectar	아가베 시럽
cream cheese	크림 치즈
feta cheese	페타 치즈
goat cheese	염소 치즈
grape seed oil	포도씨오일
hazelnut oil	헤이즐넛오일
olive oil	올리브오일
rice vinegar	쌀 식초
sherry vinegar	셰리주 식초
soy sauce	간장
walnut oil	호두오일

PINEAPPLE 파인애플

FRUIT 과일/열매	
apricot	살구
avocado	아보카도
banana	바나나
blueberry	블루베리
cranberry	크랜베리
coconut	코코넛
grapefruit	자몽
kiwi	키위
kumquat	금귤
lemon	레몬
lime	라임
melon	멜론
orange	오렌지
papaya	파파야
passion fruit	패션프루트
pomegranate	석류
raisin	건포도
strawberry	딸기

NUT 견과류	
almond	아몬드
cashewnut	캐슈넛
hazelnut	헤이즐넛
macadamia	마카다미아
peanut	땅콩
walnut	호두

LIQUEUR / WINE 리큐르 / 와인	
brandy	브랜디 (포도 발효 증류술)
cointreau	쿠앵트로 (오렌지 증류술)
grand marnier	그랑 마르니에 (오렌지 큐라소)
kirsch	키르쉬 (체리 증류술)

HERB 허브	
basil	바질
lavender	라벤더
lemongrass	레몬그라스
rosemary	로즈마리
sage	세이지
mint	민트

SPICE
향신료

black pepper	흑후추
cinnamon	시나몬
clove	정향
curry	커리
garlic	마늘
ginger	생강
nutmeg	육두구
star anise	팔각
vanilla	바닐라

OHTERS
기타

agave nectar	아가베 시럽
apple cider vinegar	사과 식초
grape seed oil	포도씨오일
olive oil	올리브오일
red wine vinegar	레드와인 식초
rice vinegar	쌀 식초
ricotta cheese	리코타 치즈
sour cream	사워 크림
white wine vinegar	화이트와인 식초

VEGETABLE
채소

beet	비트
sweet tomato	고구마
tomato	토마토

GRAIN
곡물

black bean	검은콩
brown rice	현미

PLUM 자두

FRUIT 과일/열매	
apricot	살구
banana	바나나
blackberry	블랙베리
cherry	체리
date	대추
lemon	레몬
lime	체리
nectarine	천도복숭아
orange	오렌지
passion fruit	패션프루트
peach	복숭아
raisin	건포도
raspberry	라즈베리
olive	올리브
strawberry	딸기

LIQUEUR / WINE 리큐르 / 와인	
brandy	브랜디 (포도 발효 증류술)
kirsch	키르쉬 (체리 증류술)
red wine	레드와인
rum	럼
sweet wine	스위트 와인
port wine	포트와인
white wine	화이트와인

HERB 허브	
lavender	라벤더
mint	민트
sage	세이지
parsley	파슬리

NUT 견과류	
almond	아몬드
walnut	호두

SPICE
향신료

all spice	올스파이스 (자메이카 향신료)
anise	아니스
bay leaf	월계수 잎
black pepper	흑후추
cardamom	카다멈
cinnamon	시나몬
clove	정향
coriander	고수
garlic	마늘
ginger	생강
nutmeg	육두구
vanilla	바닐라

VEGETABLE
채소

arugula	루콜라
red bell pepper	붉은 피망

GRAIN
곡물

sesame seed	참깨

OHTERS
기타

buttermilk	버터밀크
caramel	캐러멜
blue cheese	블루 치즈
cream cheese	크림 치즈
feta cheese	페타 치즈
goat cheese	염소 치즈
honey	꿀
manouri cheese	마누리 치즈
soft cheese	연질 치즈
chocolate (dark, milk, white)	초콜릿 (다크, 밀크, 화이트)
mascarpone	마스카르포네
umeboshi vinegar	매실 식초
maple syrup	메이플 시럽
olive oil	올리브오일
balsamic vinegar	발사믹 식초
champagne vinegar	샴페인 식초
red wine vinegar	레드와인 식초
yogurt	요거트

POMEGRANATE 석류

FRUIT
과일/열매

apple	사과
avocado	아보카도
banana	바나나
dried cherry	건체리
cherry	체리
coconut	코코넛
dried cranberry	건크랜베리
cranberry	크랜베리
fig	무화과
grapefruit	자몽
lime	라임
melon	멜론
nable orange	네이블 오렌지
blood orange	블러드 오렌지
pear	배
quince	모과
watermelon	수박

HERB
허브

parsley	파슬리
thyme	타임

SPICE
향신료

all spice	올스파이스 (자메이카 향신료)
cardamom	카다멈
cinnamon	시나몬
clove	정향
curry	커리
garlic	마늘
ginger	생강
mustard	겨자
sumac	옻

NUT
견과류

almond	아몬드
pecan	피칸
pinenut	잣
pistachio	피스타치오
walnut	호두

VEGETABLE
채소

arugula	루콜라
bell pepper	피망
carrot	당근
chili	고추
cucumber	오이
spinach	시금치
tomato	토마토

GRAIN 곡물	
barley	보리
chickpea	병아리콩
lentil	렌틸콩
rice	쌀

OHTERS 기타	
cream cheese	크림 치즈
goat cheese	염소 치즈
honey	꿀
olive oil	올리브오일
balsamic vinegar	발사믹 식초
sherry vinegar	셰리주 식초
red wine vinegar	레드와인 식초
white wine vinegar	화이트와인 식초
yogurt	요거트
yuzu juice	유자 주스

QUINCE 모과

FRUIT 과일/열매	
apple	사과
cherry	체리
cranberry	크랜베리
date	대추
fig	무화과
kumquat	금귤
lemon	레몬
orange	오렌지
pear	배
raisin	건포도
raspberry	라즈베리

SPICE 향신료	
black pepper	흑후추
cardamom	카다멈
clove	정향
coriander	고수
fennel	펜넬 (회향)
ginger	생강
nutmeg	육두구
star anise	팔각
vanilla	바닐라

NUT 견과류	
almond	아몬드
hazelnut	헤이즐넛
pecan	피칸
pistachio	피스타치오
walnut	호두

OHTERS 기타	
caramel	캐러멜
chili pepper	고춧가루
crème fraiche	크렘 프레슈
honey	꿀
mascarpone	마스카르포네
vinegar	식초

LIQUEUR / WINE 리큐르 / 와인	
brandy	브랜디 (포도 발효 증류술)

NOTE.

RASPBERRY 라즈베리

FRUIT 과일/열매	
apple	사과
apricot	살구
banana	바나나
blackberry	블랙베리
blueberry	블루베리
citrus	감귤류
fig	무화과
grape	포도
grapefruit	자몽
lemon	레몬
lime	라임
mango	망고
melon	멜론
nectarine	천도복숭아
orange	오렌지
papaya	파파야
peach	복숭아
pear	배
pineapple	파인애플
plum	자두
quince	모과
red currant	레드 커런트
strawberry	딸기
tangerine	귤
watermelon	수박

NUT 견과류	
hazelnut	헤이즐넛
pecan	피칸
pinenut	잣
pistachio	피스타치오

HERB 허브	
thyme	타임
verbena	버베나

SPICE 향신료	
black pepper	흑후추
cinnamon	시나몬
clove	정향
star anise	팔각
vanilla	바닐라

VEGETABLE 채소	
rhubarb	루바브

OHTERS 기타	
buttermilk	버터밀크
caramel	캐러멜
chocolate (dark, white)	초콜릿 (다크, 화이트)
crème fraiche	크렘 프레슈
goat cream	염소 치즈
honey	꿀
maple syrup	메이플 시럽
sour cream	사워 크림

STRAWBERRY 딸기

FRUIT 과일/열매	
apple	사과
apricot	살구
banana	바나나
blackberry	블랙베리
blueberry	블루베리
cantaloup melon	캔털루프 멜론
coconut	코코넛
fig	무화과
kiwi	키위
grapefruit	자몽
guava	구아바
lemon	레몬
lime	라임
mango	망고
melon	멜론
orange	오렌지
papaya	파파야
passion fruit	패션프루트
peach	복숭아
pineapple	파인애플
plum	자두
pomegranate	석류
raspberry	라즈베리
watermelon	수박

NUT 견과류	
almond	아몬드
hazelnut	헤이즐넛
pecan	피칸
pinenut	잣
pistachio	피스타치오
walnut	호두

LIQUEUR / WINE 리큐르 / 와인	
cointreau	쿠앵트로 (오렌지 증류술)
curacao	큐라소
framboise liqueur	딸기 리큐르
masala wine	마살라 와인
port wine	포트 와인
rose wine	로제 와인
rum	럼
sherry	셰리주
sweet wine	스위트 와인

HERB 허브	
basil	바질
mint	민트
thyme	타임

SPICE
향신료

black pepper	흑후추
red pepper	레드페퍼
cinnamon	시나몬
fennel	펜넬 (회향)
ginger	생강
vanilla	바닐라

VEGETABLE
채소

rhubarb	루바브
spinach	시금치
tomato	토마토

GRAIN
곡물

oat	오트

OHTERS
기타

agave nectar	아가베 시럽
almond milk	아몬드 밀크
brown sugar	황설탕
buttermilk	버터밀크
caramel	캐러멜
cream	생크림
crème fraiche	크렘 프레슈
burrata cheese	부라타 치즈
cream cheese	크림 치즈
feta cheese	페타 치즈
goat cheese	염소 치즈
mozzarella cheese	모차렐라 치즈
ricotta cheese	리코타 치즈
sheep's milk cheese	양젖 치즈
dark chocolate	다크초콜릿
honey	꿀
maple syrup	메이플 시럽
mascarpone	마스카르포네
olive oil	올리브오일
sour cream	사워 크림
red wine vinegar	레드와인 식초
balsamic vinegar	발사믹 식초
yogurt	요거트

WATERMELON 수박

FRUIT
과일/열매

blackberry	블랙베리
blueberry	블루베리
cranberry	크랜베리
cantaloup melon	캔털루프 멜론
lemon	레몬
lime	라임
orange	오렌지
raspberry	라즈베리
strawberry	딸기

NUT
건과류

almond	아몬드
pistachio	피스타치오

HERB
허브

basil	바질
mint	민트
parsley	파슬리
rosemary	로즈마리

VEGETABLE
채소

arugula	루콜라
chili	고추
cucumber	오이
tomato	토마토

SPICE
향신료

black pepper	흑후추
coriander	고수
fennel	펜넬 (회향)
vanilla	바닐라

GRAIN
곡물

black sesame seed	흑임자
black sesame	검은깨

OHTERS
기타

agave nectar	아가베 시럽
honey	꿀
blue cheese	블루 치즈
feta cheese	페타 치즈
goat cheese	염소 치즈
ricotta cheese	리코타 치즈
black balsamic vinegar	블랙 발사믹 식초
white balsamic vinegar	화이트 발사믹 식초
raspberry vinegar	라즈베리 식초
red wine vinegar	레드와인 식초
rice wine vinegar	막걸리 식초
sherry vinegar	셰리주 식초
yogurt	요거트

YUZA 유자

FRUIT 과일/열매	
banana	바나나
pomegranate	석류

LIQUEUR / WINE 리큐르 / 와인	
mirin	미림 (맛술)

VEGETABLE 채소	
chili	고추

GRAIN 곡물	
sesame seed	참깨

OHTERS 기타	
cream cheese	크림 치즈
miso	미소 (일본식 된장)
canola oil	카놀라오일
grape seed oil	포도씨오일
olive oil	올리브오일
vegetable oil	식용유
soy sauce	간장
tapioca	타피오카
rice vinegar	쌀 식초

ALMOND 아몬드

FRUIT
과일/열매

apple	사과
apricot	살구
banana	바나나
blackberry	블랙베리
black currant	블랙 커런트
blueberry	블루베리
date	대추
cherry	체리
coconut	코코넛
cranberry	크랜베리
fig	무화과
grape	포도
lemon	레몬
lime	라임
nectarine	천도복숭아
orange	오렌지
passion fruit	패션프루트
peach	복숭아
pear	배
plum	자두
raisin	건포도
raspberry	라즈베리
red currant	레드 커런트
strawberry	딸기

NUT
견과류

hazelnut	헤이즐넛
pecan	피칸
pinenut	잣
pistachio	피스타치오
walnut	호두

LIQUEUR / WINE
리큐르 / 와인

amaretto	아마레토
brandy	브랜디 (포도 발효 증류술)
orange liqueur	오렌지 리큐르
rum	럼

HERB
허브

lavender	라벤더
thyme	타임
rosemary	로즈마리

SPICE
향신료

black pepper	흑후추
cardamom	카다멈
cayenne	카이엔
cinnamon	시나몬
coffee	커피
curry	커리
garlic	마늘
ginger	생강
vanilla	바닐라

VEGETABLE
채소

bell pepper	피망
carrot	당근
paprika	파프리카
rhubarb	루바브
tomato	토마토

GRAIN
곡물

barley	보리
oat	오트
rice	쌀
green bean	깍지콩
corn meal	옥수수가루
sweet rice	찹쌀

OHTERS
기타

butter	버터
butterscotch	버터스카치 (스카치 캔디)
brown sugar	황설탕
caramel	캐러멜
cacao nibs	카카오닙스
chili powder	고춧가루
chocolate (dark, milk, white)	초콜릿 (다크, 밀크, 화이트)
cacao	카카오
cream	생크림
champagne vinegar	샴페인 식초
honey	꿀
maple syrup	메이플 시럽
mascarpone	마스카르포네
milk	우유
olive oil	올리브오일
rose water	장미수
sea salt	바닷소금
sherry vinegar	셰리주 식초
blue cheese	블루 치즈
cream cheese	크림 치즈
goat cheese	염소 치즈
ricotta cheese	리코타 치즈
manchego cheese	만체고 치즈
romano cheese	로마노 치즈
stilton cheese	스틸턴 치즈
yogurt	요거트

CASHEWNUT 캐슈넛

FRUIT
과일/열매

apricot	살구
banana	바나나
blueberry	블루베리
coconut	코코넛
date	대추
grapefruit	자몽
guava	구아바
lemon	레몬
lime	라임
mango	망고
papaya	파파야
passion fruit	패션프루트
persimmon	감
pineapple	파인애플

NUT
견과류

almond	아몬드
macadamia	마카다미아
pinenut	잣
hazelnut	헤이즐넛

LIQUEUR / WINE
리큐르 / 와인

rum	럼

HERB
허브

mint	민트
thyme	타임

SPICE
향신료

black pepper	흑후추
cardamom	카다멈
cayenne	카이엔
cinnamon	시나몬
coffee	커피
clove	정향
curry	커리
garlic	마늘
ginger	생강
nutmeg	육두구
wasabi	와사비
vanilla	바닐라

VEGETABLE
채소

bell pepper	피망
pumpkin	호박
tomato	토마토
spinach	시금치

GRAIN 곡물	
basmati rice	바스마티 쌀 (인도의 쌀)
corn	옥수수
green bean	깍지콩
jasmin rice	재스민 쌀 (태국의 쌀)
sesame seed	참깨
wheat berry	밀알

OHTERS 기타	
brown sugar	황설탕
butter	버터
cacao nibs	카카오닙스
chocolate (dark, milk, white)	초콜릿 (다크, 밀크, 화이트)
goat cheese	염소 치즈
honey	꿀
maple syrup	매이플 시럽
miso	미소 (일본식 된장)
olive oil	올리브오일
peanut butter	땅콩 버터
cream	생크림
sea salt	바닷소금
sour cream	사워 크림

HAZELNUT 헤이즐넛

FRUIT 과일/열매	
apple	사과
apricot	살구
dried apricot	건살구
banana	바나나
blackberry	블랙베리
blueberry	블루베리
cherry	체리
chestnut	밤
cranberry	크랜베리
date	대추
fig	무화과
grape	포도
grapefruit	자몽
lemon	레몬
mango	망고
mandarin orange	만다린 오렌지
nectarine	천도복숭아
orange	오렌지
passion fruit	패션프루트
peach	복숭아
pear	배
persimmon	감
pineapple	파인애플
plum	자두
prune	건자두
raspberry	라즈베리
raisin	건포도
strawberry	딸기

NUT 견과류	
almond	아몬드
pecan	피칸
walnut	호두

LIQUEUR / WINE 리큐르 / 와인	
almond liqueur	아몬드 리큐르
cognac	코냑
rum	럼
red wine	레드와인

HERB 허브	
mint	민트
parsley	파슬리
rosemary	로즈마리

SPICE 향신료	
cinnamon	시나몬
coffee	커피
fennel	펜넬 (회향)
ginger	생강
vanilla	바닐라

VEGETABLE 채소	
asparagus	아스파라거스
beet	비트
kale	케일
pumpkin	호박
spinach	시금치

OHTERS 기타	
buttermilk	버터밀크
blue cheese	블루 치즈
brown sugar	황설탕
feta cheese	페타 치즈
goat cheese	염소 치즈
gorgonzola cheese	고르곤졸라 치즈
manchego cheese	만체고 치즈
ricotta cheese	리코타 치즈
taleggio cheese	탈레지오 치즈
gruyere cheese	그뤼에르 치즈
caramel	캐러멜
chocolate (dark, milk, white)	초콜릿 (다크, 밀크, 화이트)
cream cheese	크림 치즈
hazelnut oil	헤이즐넛오일
orange oil	오렌지오일
granola	그래놀라
morel	모렐 (곰보버섯)
wild mushroom	야생버섯
honey	꿀
maple syrup	메이플 시럽
mascarpone	마스카르포네
balsamic vinegar	발사믹 식초
champagne vinegar	샴페인 식초
sherry vinegar	셰리주 식초
white wine vinegar	화이트와인 식초

MACADAMIA 마카다미아

FRUIT
과일/열매

apricot	살구
banana	바나나
coconut	코코넛
date	대추
fig	무화과
grapefruit	자몽
guava	구아바
lemon	레몬
lime	라임
mango	망고
orange	오렌지
papaya	파파야
passion fruit	패션프루트
peach	복숭아
pineapple	파인애플
prune	건자두
raspberry	라즈베리

HERB
허브

mint	민트

SPICE
향신료

coffee	커피
ginger	생강

OHTERS
기타

caramel	캐러멜
chocolate (dark, milk, white)	초콜릿 (다크, 밀크, 화이트)
goat cheese	염소 치즈
honey	꿀
maple syrup	메이플 시럽

NUT
견과류

cashewnut	캐슈넛

LIQUEUR / WINE
리큐르 / 와인

rum	럼

NOTE.

PEANUT 땅콩

FRUIT 과일/열매	
apple	사과
banana	바나나
coconut	코코넛
grape	포도
lemon	레몬
lime	라임
mango	망고
pear	배
raspberry	라즈베리
raisin	건포도
strawberry	딸기

SPICE 향신료	
black pepper	흑후추
coffee	커피
cinnamon	시나몬
clove	정향
coriander	고수
curry	커리
garlic	마늘
ginger	생강
turmeric	강황
vanilla	바닐라

HERB 허브	
basil	바질
lemongrass	레몬그라스
mint	민트

VEGETABLE 채소	
arugula	루콜라
carrot	당근
chili	고추
cucumber	오이
paprika	파프리카
pumpkin	호박
tomato	토마토
sweet potato	고구마

GRAIN 곡물	
green bean	깍지콩
oat	오트
rice	쌀
sesame seed	참깨

OHTERS 기타	
agave nectar	아가베 시럽
apple cider vinegar	사과 식초
brown rice vinegar	현미 식초
caramel	캐러멜
chocolate (dark, milk, white)	초콜릿 (다크, 밀크, 화이트)
honey	꿀
olive oil	올리브오일
peanut oil	땅콩오일
red wine vinegar	레드와인 식초
rice wine vinegar	막걸리 식초
sunflower seed oil	해바라기씨오일
sesame seed oil	참기름
soy sauce	간장
vegetable oil	식물성오일

PECAN 피칸

FRUIT 과일/열매	
apple	사과
apricot	살구
banana	바나나
blackberry	블랙베리
black currant	블랙 커런트
blueberry	블루베리
cherry	체리
dried cranberry	건크랜베리
date	대추
fig	무화과
grape	포도
grapefruit	자몽
kumquat	금귤
lemon	레몬
nectarine	천도복숭아
orange	오렌지
peach	복숭아
pear	배
persimmon	감
pineapple	파인애플
plum	자두
pomegranate	석류
prune	건자두
quince	모과
raisin	건포도
raspberry	라즈베리
strawberry	딸기

NUT 견과류	
almond	아몬드
hazelnut	헤이즐넛

LIQUEUR / WINE 리큐르 / 와인	
bourbon	버번 (위스키)
brandy	브랜디 (포도 발효 증류술)
red wine	레드와인
rum	럼

HERB 허브	
parsley	파슬리

SPICE 향신료	
cinnamon	시나몬
ginger	생강
garlic	마늘
nutmeg	육두구
star anise	팔각
vanilla	바닐라

VEGETABLE 채소	
paprika	파프리카
sweet tomato	고구마

GRAIN 곡물	
oat	오트

OHTERS 기타	
brown butter	브라운 버터
blue cheese	블루 치즈
goat cheese	염소 치즈
granola	그래놀라
maple syrup	메이플 시럽
ricotta cheese	리코타 치즈
yogurt	요거트

PINENUT 잣

FRUIT
과일/열매

apple	사과
apricot	살구
cranberry	크랜베리
currant	커런트
fig	무화과
lemon	레몬
nectarine	천도복숭아
orange	오렌지
peach	복숭아
pear	배
plum	자두
prune	건자두
raisin	건포도
raspberry	라즈베리

NUT
견과류

almond	아몬드
pistachio	피스타치오

LIQUEUR / WINE
리큐르 / 와인

red wine	레드와인
rum	럼

HERB
허브

basil	바질
parsley	파슬리
rosemary	로즈마리
sage	세이지

SPICE
향신료

anise	아니스
fennel	펜넬 (회향)
garlic	마늘
saffron	사프란
vanilla	바닐라

VEGETABLE
채소

beet	비트
carrot	당근
sweet tomato	고구마
tomato	토마토

GRAIN
곡물

green bean	깍지콩

OHTERS 기타	
caramel	캐러멜
feta cheese	페타 치즈
goat cheese	염소 치즈
honey	꿀
maple syrup	메이플 시럽
mascarpone	마스카르포네
mozzarella cheese	모차렐라 치즈
olive oil	올리브오일
parmesan cheese	파르메산 치즈
pinenut oil	잣오일
ricotta cheese	리코타 치즈
walnut oil	호두오일

PISTACHIO 피스타치오

FRUIT 과일/열매	
apple	사과
apricot	살구
avocado	아보카도
banana	바나나
coconut	코코넛
cranberry	크랜베리
currant	커런트
date	대추
fig	무화과
grape	포도
grapefruit	자몽
kumquat	금귤
lemon	레몬
lime	라임
mango	망고
melon	멜론
nectarine	천도복숭아
orange	오렌지
peach	복숭아
pear	배
pineapple	파인애플
plum	자두
pomegranate	석류
prune	건자두
quince	모과
raspberry	라즈베리
watermelon	수박

NUT 견과류	
pinenut	잣
walnut	호두

HERB 허브	
basil	바질
lemongrass	레몬그라스
mint	민트

SPICE 향신료	
ginger	생강
garlic	마늘
saffron	사프란

VEGETABLE 채소	
beet	비트
carrot	당근
tomato	토마토
watercress	물냉이

GRAIN 곡물	
corn meal	옥수수가루
lentil	렌틸콩
quinoa	퀴노아

OHTERS 기타	
blue cheese	블루 치즈
chili powder	고춧가루
chocolate (dark, white)	초콜릿 (다크, 화이트)
goat cheese	염소 치즈
gorgonzola	고르곤졸라 치즈
maple syrup	메이플 시럽
oatmeal	오트밀
parmesan cheese	파르메산 치즈
raspberry vinegar	라즈베리 식초
ricotta cheese	리코타 치즈
rose water	장미수
taleggio cheese	탈레지오 치즈
yogurt	요거트

WALNUT 호두

FRUIT 과일/열매	
apple	사과
apricot	살구
blueberry	블루베리
banana	바나나
cherry	체리
coconut	코코넛
cranberry	크랜베리
currant	커런트
date	대추
fig	무화과
grape	포도
grapefruit	자몽
kumquat	금귤
lemon	레몬
nectarine	천도복숭아
orange	오렌지
peach	복숭아
pear	배
plum	자두
quince	모과
raisin	건포도

LIQUEUR / WINE 리큐르 / 와인	
madeira wine	마데이라 와인 (강화 와인)
port wine	포트 와인
rum	럼
sherry wine	셰리 와인
sweet wine	스위트 와인

HERB 허브	
basil	바질
thyme	타임
parsley	파슬리
sage	세이지

SPICE 향신료	
cinnamon	시나몬
coffee	커피
fennel	펜넬 (회향)
garlic	마늘
nutmeg	육두구

NUT 견과류	
cashewnut	캐슈넛
hazelnut	헤이즐넛

VEGETABLE
채소

beet	비트
carrot	당근
parsnip	파스닙
pumpkin	호박
spinach	시금치
sweet potato	고구마
sun dried tomato	선드라이 토마토
tomato	토마토

GRAIN
곡물

fava bean	누에콩
green bean	깍지콩
oat	오트
quinoa	퀴노아
rice	쌀
white bean	흰 강낭콩

OHTERS
기타

blue cheese	블루 치즈
camembert cheese	카망베르 치즈
caramel	캐러멜
cheddar cheese	체더 치즈
chocolate (dark, milk, white)	초콜릿 (다크, 밀크, 화이트)
cream cheese	크림 치즈
feta cheese	페타 치즈
goat cheese	염소 치즈
gorgonzola cheese	고르곤졸라 치즈
manchego cheese	만체고 치즈
maple syrup	메이플 시럽
mascarpone	마스카르포네
monterey jack cheese	몬터레이 잭 치즈
olive oil	올리브오일
parmesan cheese	파르메산 치즈
pecorino cheese	페코리노 치즈
ricotta cheese	리코타 치즈
roquefort cheese	로크포르 치즈
sheep's milk cheese	양젖 치즈
sherry vinegar	셰리주 식초
stilton cheese	스틸턴 치즈
porcini mushroom	포르치니 버섯
yogurt	요거트

BASIL 바질

FRUIT
과일/열매

apple	사과
apricot	살구
avocado	아보카도
blueberry	블루베리
coconut	코코넛
grapefruit	자몽
lemon	레몬
lime	라임
nectarine	천도복숭아
orange	오렌지
peach	복숭아
pineapple	파인애플
raspberry	라즈베리
strawberry	딸기
watermelon	수박

NUT
견과류

almond	아몬드
hazelnut	헤이즐넛
peanut	땅콩
pinenut	잣
pistachio	피스타치오

LIQUEUR / WINE
리큐르 / 와인

rum	럼
red wine	레드와인

HERB
허브

mint	민트
lemongrass	레몬그라스
parsley	파슬리
rosemary	로즈마리
oregano	오레가노

SPICE
향신료

black pepper	흑후추
cinnamon	시나몬
coriander	고수
curry	커리
garlic	마늘
ginger	생강
marjoram	마조람
vanilla	바닐라
white pepper	백후추

VEGETABLE
채소

bell pepper	피망
cucumber	오이
spinach	시금치
sweet potato	고구마
tomato	토마토

GRAIN
곡물

cannellini bean	카넬리니콩
chickpea	병아리콩
corn	옥수수
fava bean	누에콩
green bean	깍지콩
quinoa	퀴노아
rice	쌀

OHTERS
기타

artichoke	아티초크
balsamic vinegar	발사믹 식초
feta cheese	페타 치즈
fresh white cheese	프레시 화이트 치즈
goat cheese	염소 치즈
mozzarella cheese	모차렐라 치즈
olive oil	올리브오일
ricotta cheese	리코타 치즈
parmesan cheese	파르메산 치즈
pecorino cheese	페코리노 치즈
sherry vinegar	셰리주 식초

CORIANDER 고수

FRUIT 과일/열매	
apricot	살구
avocado	아보카도
blackberry	블랙베리
cantaloupe melon	캔털루프 멜론
cherry	체리
coconut	코코넛
fig	무화과
lemon	레몬
lime	라임
mango	망고
nectarine	천도복숭아
orange	오렌지
papaya	파파야
peach	복숭아
plum	자두
raspberry	라즈베리
strawberry	딸기

NUT 견과류	
almond	아몬드
pumpkin seed	호박씨

HERB 허브	
basil	바질
lemongrass	레몬그라스
mint	민트
parsley	파슬리

SPICE 향신료	
cardamom	카다멈
chutney	처트니 (인도 조미료)
cinnamon	시나몬
curry	커리
garlic	마늘
ginger	생강

VEGETABLE 채소	
carrot	당근
chili	고추
cucumber	오이
edamame	풋콩

GRAIN 곡물	
black bean	검은콩
chickpea	병아리콩
corn	옥수수
fava bean	누에콩
pinto bean	핀토빈
lentil	렌틸콩
white bean	흰 강낭콩
quinoa	퀴노아

OHTERS 기타	
coconut milk	코코넛 밀크
miso	미소 (일본식 된장)
olive oil	올리브오일
white wine vinegar	화이트와인 식초

LAVENDER 라벤더

FRUIT 과일/열매	
apple	사과
apricot	살구
blackberry	블랙베리
blueberry	블루베리
cherry	체리
coconut	코코넛
fig	무화과
guava	구아바
lemon	레몬
mango	망고
nectarine	천도복숭아
orange	오렌지
peach	복숭아
plum	자두
raspberry	라즈베리
rhubarb	루바브
strawberry	딸기

HERB 허브	
basil	바질
rosemary	로즈마리
thyme	타임

SPICE 향신료	
caraway	캐러웨이
cinnamon	시나몬
ginger	생강
saffron	사프란
vanilla	바닐라

VEGETABLE 채소	
carrot	당근
edamame	풋콩
watercress	물냉이

NUT 견과류	
walnut	호두
pumpkin seed	호박씨

GRAIN 곡물	
black bean	검은콩
chickpea	병아리콩
corn	옥수수
fava bean	누에콩
pinto bean	핀토빈
lentil	렌틸콩
white bean	흰 강낭콩
quinoa	퀴노아

OHTERS 기타	
black tea	홍차
blue cheese	블루 치즈
cream	생크림
crème fraiche	크렘 프레슈
fromage blanc cheese	프로마주 블랑 치즈
goat cheese	염소 치즈
gorgonzola cheese	고르곤졸라 치즈
olive oil	올리브오일
sugar powder	슈거파우더
walnut oil	호두오일
white wine vinegar	화이트와인 식초
yogurt	요거트

LEMONGRASS 레몬그라스

FRUIT
과일/열매

cherry	체리
coconut	코코넛
guava	구아바
lemon	레몬
lime	라임
pineapple	파인애플
raspberry	라즈베리
strawberry	딸기

VEGETABLE
채소

carrot	당근
chili	고추
tomato	토마토

GRAIN
곡물

corn	옥수수

HERB
허브

basil	바질
mint	민트

OHTERS
기타

black tea	홍차
honey	꿀
sesame seed oil	참기름
shiitake mushroom	표고버섯
soy sauce	간장
rice vinegar	쌀 식초
yogurt	요거트

SPICE
향신료

cinnamon	시나몬
clove	정향
coriander	고수
garlic	마늘
ginger	생강
tamarind	타마린드
turmeric	강황
vanilla	바닐라

NOTE.

MINT 민트

FRUIT 과일/열매	
apple	사과
apricot	살구
blueberry	블루베리
coconut	코코넛
fig	무화과
grape	포도
grapefruit	자몽
green papaya	그린 파파야
honeydew melon	허니듀 멜론
lemon	레몬
lime	라임
lychee	리치
mango	망고
melon	멜론
nectarine	천도복숭아
olive	올리브
orange	오렌지
peaches	복숭아
pear	배
plum	자두
pineapple	파인애플
raspberry	라즈베리
strawberry	딸기
watermelon	수박

NUT 견과류	
almond	아몬드
cashewnut	캐슈넛
pinenut	잣
pistachio	피스타치오

LIQUEUR / WINE 리큐르 / 와인	
bourbon	버번 (위스키)
gin	진
wine	와인

HERB 허브	
basil	바질
dill	딜
lemongrass	레몬그라스
parsley	파슬리
lavender	라벤더

SPICE
향신료

cardamom	카다멈
cinnamon	시나몬
coriander	고수
curry	커리
garlic	마늘
ginger	생강
vanilla	바닐라

VEGETABLE
채소

carrot	당근
spinach	시금치

GRAIN
곡물

black bean	검은콩
green bean	깍지콩
white bean	흰 강낭콩
chickpea	병아리콩
lentil	렌틸콩
quinoa	퀴노아

OHTERS
기타

balsamic vinegar	발사믹 식초
chocolate (dark, white)	초콜릿 (다크, 화이트)
chevre cheese	염소젖 치즈
feta cheese	페타 치즈
honey	꿀
ricotta cheese	리코타 치즈
white vinegar	화이트 식초
yogurt	요거트

ROSEMARY 로즈마리

FRUIT
과일/열매

apple	사과
apricot	살구
grapefruit	자몽
grape	포도
fig	무화과
lemon	레몬
lime	라임
olive	올리브
orange	오렌지
pear	배
strawberry	딸기

LIQUEUR / WINE
리큐르 / 와인

gin	진
sherry	셰리주

HERB
허브

lavender	라벤더
lovage	러비지
marjoram	마조람
mint	민트
thyme	타임
oregano	오레가노
parsley	파슬리

SPICE
향신료

bay leaf	월계수 잎
black pepper	흑후추
fennel	펜넬 (회향)

VEGETABLE
채소

beet	비트
carrot	당근
parsnip	파스닙
spinach	시금치
sweet potato	고구마
tomato	토마토

GRAIN
곡물

barley	보리
cannellini bean	카넬리니콩
dried bean	건조콩
fava bean	누에콩
green bean	깍지콩
quinoa	퀴노아

OHTERS 기타	
butter	버터
cheddar cheese	체더 치즈
chevre cheese	염소젖 치즈
cream cheese	크림 치즈
feta cheese	페타 치즈
goat cheese	염소 치즈
parmesan cheese	파르메산 치즈
ricotta cheese	리코타 치즈
honey	꿀
milk	우유
mushroom	버섯
oil	식용유
balsamic vinegar	발사믹 식초
red wine vinegar	레드와인 식초
yogurt	요거트

SAFFRON 사프란

FRUIT 과일/열매	
lemon	레몬
orange	오렌지
raisin	건포도

VEGETABLE 채소	
potato	감자
roasted bell pepper	로스팅한 피망
tomato	토마토

HERB 허브	
basil	바질
marjoram	마조람

OHTERS 기타	
butter	버터
rose water	장미수
yogurt	요거트

SPICE 향신료	
black pepper	흑후추
cardamom	카다멈
cayenne	카이엔
cinnamon	시나몬
curry	커리
fennel	펜넬 (회향)
garlic	마늘
ginger	생강
vanilla	바닐라

THYME 타임

FRUIT
과일/열매

apple	사과
apricot	살구
lemon	레몬
melon	멜론
orange	오렌지
pear	배
raspberry	라즈베리

HERB
허브

basil	바질
rosemary	로즈마리
mint	민트
oregano	오레가노
parsley	파슬리

SPICE
향신료

bay leaf	월계수 잎
black pepper	흑후추
garlic	마늘

VEGETABLE
채소

beet	비트
carrot	당근
spinach	시금치

GRAIN
곡물

black bean	검은콩
corn	옥수수
green bean	깍지콩
kidney bean	강낭콩
pinto bean	핀토빈
quinoa	퀴노아

OHTERS
기타

blue cheese	블루 치즈
cheddar cheese	체더 치즈
dark chocolate	다크초콜릿
fresh cheese	프레시 치즈
goat cheese	염소 치즈
mushroom	버섯
olive oil	올리브오일
ricotta cheese	리코타 치즈
yogurt	요거트

ALLSPICE 올스파이스 (시나몬, 정향, 육두구를 섞은 향)

FRUIT
과일/열매

apple	사과
banana	바나나
coconut	코코넛
mango	망고
pear	배
peach	복숭아
pineapple	파인애플
red currant	레드 커런트

SPICE
향신료

black pepper	흑후추
cinnamon	시나몬
clove	정향
coriander	고수
curry	커리
ginger	생강
nutmeg	육두구
mace	메이스 (향신료의 일종)

NUT
견과류

pecan	피칸

VEGETABLE
채소

beet	비트
carrot	당근
cucumber	오이
pumpkin	호박
sweet potato	고구마

LIQUEUR / WINE
리큐르 / 와인

red wine	레드와인
rum	럼

OHTERS
기타

apple cider vinegar	사과 식초
cacao	카카오
red wine vinegar	레드와인 식초

GRAIN
곡물

baked bean	구운 콩
black bean	검은콩
quinoa	퀴노아

NOTE.

ANISE 아니스

FRUIT 과일/열매	
apple	사과
chestnut	밤
cranberry	크랜베리
coconut	코코넛
date	대추
lemon	레몬
melon	멜론
mango	망고
orange	오렌지
pear	배
peach	복숭아
pineapple	파인애플
plum	자두
quince	모과
raisin	건포도
strawberry	딸기
fig	무화과

LIQUEUR / WINE 리큐르 / 와인	
rum	럼
red wine	레드와인

SPICE 향신료	
allspice	올스파이스 (자메이카 향신료)
black pepper	흑후추
cardamom	카다멈
cinnamon	시나몬
clove	정향
coffee	커피
coriander	고수
curry	커리
fennel	펜넬 (회향)
garlic	마늘
ginger	생강
nutmeg	육두구
mace	메이스 (향신료의 일종)
vanilla	바닐라
star anise	팔각

NUT 견과류	
almond	아몬드
hazelnut	헤이즐넛
pinenut	잣
walnut	호두

VEGETABLE 채소	
rhubarb	루바브
beet	비트
carrot	당근
tomato	토마토
sweet potato	고구마
pumpkin	호박

GRAIN 곡물	
baked bean	구운 콩
black bean	검은콩
lentil	렌틸콩
quinoa	퀴노아
rice	쌀

OHTERS 기타	
cream	생크림
goat cheese	염소 치즈
maple syrup	메이플 시럽
munster cheese	뮌스터 치즈
pickle	피클
ricotta cheese	리코타 치즈
red wine vinegar	레드와인 식초

CINNAMON 시나몬

FRUIT
과일/열매

apple	사과
apricot	살구
banana	바나나
blackberry	블랙베리
blood orange	블러드 오렌지
blueberry	블루베리
cherry	체리
coconut	코코넛
date	대추
fig	무화과
grapefruit	자몽
lemon	레몬
nectarine	천도복숭아
orange	오렌지
peach	복숭아
pear	배
plum	자두
raisin	건포도

NUT
견과류

almond	아몬드
pecan	피칸

LIQUEUR / WINE
리큐르 / 와인

red wine	레드와인

SPICE
향신료

anise	아니스
black pepper	흑후추
cardamom	카다멈
clove	정향
curry powder	커리 파우더
coffee	커피
garam masala	가람 마살라
ginger	생강
nutmeg	육두구
tamarind	타마린드
vanilla	바닐라

VEGETABLE
채소

beet	비트
carrot	당근
chili	고추
pumpkin	호박
rhubarb	루바브
sweet potato	고구마
tomato	토마토

 **SESAME SEED** 참깨

GRAIN 곡물	
corn	옥수수
oat	오트
rice	쌀

FRUIT 과일/열매	
apple	사과
banana	바나나
lemon	레몬

OHTERS 기타	
black tea	홍차
brown sugar	황설탕
butter	버터
caramel	캐러멜
chocolate (dark, milk, white)	초콜릿 (다크, 밀크, 화이트)
milk	우유
cream cheese	크림 치즈
honey	꿀
maple syrup	메이플 시럽
oatmeal	오트밀
rose water	장미수
yogurt	요거트

SPICE 향신료	
ginger	생강
vanilla	바닐라

CARROT 당근

FRUIT 과일/열매	
apple	사과
apricot	살구
avocado	아보카도
coconut	코코넛
date	대추
pineapple	파인애플
lemon	레몬
lime	라임
orange	오렌지
raisin	건포도

NUT 견과류	
almond	아몬드
cashewnut	캐슈넛
hazelnut	헤이즐넛
walnut	호두

LIQUEUR / WINE 리큐르 / 와인	
brandy	브랜디 (포도 발효 증류술)
rum	럼

HERB 허브	
basil	바질
chervil	처빌
dill	딜
rosemary	로즈마리
mint	민트

SPICE 향신료	
allspice	올스파이스 (자메이카 향신료)
bay leaf	월계수 잎
black pepper	흑후추
caraway	캐러웨이
cardamom	카다멈
clove	정향
cinnamon	시나몬
coriander	고수
curry	커리
fennel	펜넬 (회향)
garlic	마늘
ginger	생강
nutmeg	육두구
marjoram	마조람
star anise	팔각
tamarind	타마린드

VEGETABLE
채소

beet	비트
chili	고추
cucumber	오이
parsnip	파스닙
paprika	파프리카

GRAIN
곡물

chickpea	병아리콩
lentil	렌틸콩
sesame seed	참깨

OHTERS
기타

brown butter	브라운 버터
brown sugar	황설탕
crème fraiche	크렘 프레슈
honey	꿀
maple syrup	메이플 시럽
mascarpone	마스카르포네
miso	미소 (일본식 된장)
olive oil	올리브오일
peanut butter	땅콩 버터

GINGER 생강

FRUIT 과일/열매	
agave	아가베
apple	사과
apricot	살구
banana	바나나
blueberry	블루베리
coconut	코코넛
cherry	체리
cranberry	크랜베리
fig	무화과
grape	포도
grapefruit	자몽
kiwi	키위
kumquat	금귤
lemon	레몬
lime	라임
lychee	리치
mango	망고
melon	멜론
nectarine	천도복숭아
orange	오렌지
papaya	파파야
passion fruit	패션프루트
peach	복숭아
pear	배
persimmon	감
pineapple	파인애플
plum	자두

prune	건자두
raisin	건포도
raspberry	라즈베리
strawberry	딸기

NUT 견과류	
almond	아몬드
hazelnut	헤이즐넛
macadamia	마카다미아
peanut	땅콩
cashewnut	캐슈넛

HERB 허브	
basil	바질
lavender	라벤더
lemongrass	레몬그라스
mint	민트

GRAIN 곡물	
chickpea	병아리콩
corn	옥수수
lentil	렌틸콩
sesame seed	참깨
snow pea	깍지완두

SPICE
향신료

anise	아니스
cardamom	카다멈
cinnamon	시나몬
clove	정향
coriander	고수
curry	커리
fennel	펜넬 (회향)
garam masala	가람 마살라
garlic	마늘
star anise	팔각
tamarind	타마린드
turmeric	강황
vanilla	바닐라
wasabi	와사비

VEGETABLE
채소

carrot	당근
chili	고추
edamame	풋콩
parsnip	파스닙
pumpkin	호박
rhubarb	루바브
spinach	시금치
sweet potato	고구마
tomato	토마토

LIQUEUR / WINE
리큐르 / 와인

rum	럼
mirin	미림 (맛술)
sake	사케

OHTERS
기타

black tea	홍차
caramel	캐러멜
chocolate (dark, milk, white)	초콜릿 (다크, 밀크, 화이트)
honey	꿀
kombu	다시마
maple syrup	메이플 시럽
miso	미소 (일본식 된장)
grape seed oil	포도씨오일
sesame seed oil	참기름
soy sauce	간장
apple cider vinegar	사과 식초
brown rice vinegar	현미 식초
champagne vinegar	샴페인 식초
rice wine vinegar	막걸리 식초
sherry vinegar	셰리주 식초
white wine vinegar	화이트와인 식초
yogurt	요거트

 **PUMPKIN** 호박

FRUIT 과일/열매	
apple	사과
coconut	코코넛
cranberry	크랜베리
kumquat	금귤
lemon	레몬
lime	라임
orange	오렌지
pear	서양배
pineapple	파인애플
plum	자두
quince	모과
raisin	건포도

NUT 견과류	
almond	아몬드
cashewnut	캐슈넛
hazelnut	헤이즐넛
peanut	땅콩
pecan	피칸
pinenut	잣
walnut	호두

LIQUEUR / WINE 리큐르 / 와인	
brandy	브랜디 (포도 발효 증류술)
cognac	코냑

HERB 허브	
basil	바질
lemongrass	레몬그라스
parsley	파슬리
mint	민트

SPICE 향신료	
allspice	올스파이스 (자메이카 향신료)
bay leaf	월계수 잎
black pepper	흑후추
cardamom	카다멈
cinnamon	시나몬
clove	정향
coriander	고수
fennel	펜넬 (회향)
garlic	마늘
ginger	생강
nutmeg	육두구
vanilla	바닐라

VEGETABLE 채소	
carrot	당근
chili	고추
parsnip	파스닙

GRAIN 곡물	
chickpea	병아리콩
corn	옥수수
oat	오트

OHTERS 기타	
caramel	캐러멜
chocolate (dark, milk, white)	초콜릿 (다크, 밀크, 화이트)
cream cheese	크림 치즈
honey	꿀
maple syrup	메이플 시럽
miso	미소 (일본식 된장)
molasses	당밀
mushroom	버섯
oatmeal	오트밀
parmesan cheese	파르메산 치즈
sour cream	사워 크림

RHUBARB 루바브

FRUIT 과일/열매	
apple	사과
apricot	살구
banana	바나나
blackberry	블랙베리
blueberry	블루베리
cherry	체리
coconut	코코넛
grapefruit	포도
lemon	레몬
lime	라임
mango	망고
nectarine	천도복숭아
orange	오렌지
peach	복숭아
pineapple	파인애플
pomegranate	석류
plum	자두
raisin	건포도
raspberry	라즈베리
strawberry	딸기

NUT 견과류	
almond	아몬드
hazelnut	헤이즐넛
pistachio	피스타치오

LIQUEUR / WINE 리큐르 / 와인	
champagne	샴페인
red wine	레드와인
sparkling wine	스파클링 와인
sweet wine	스위트 와인

NOTE.

CORN 옥수수

FRUIT
과일/열매

avocado	아보카도
blackberry	블랙베리
blueberry	블루베리
lemon	레몬
lime	라임
nectarine	천도복숭아
raspberry	라즈베리

NUT
견과류

pinenut	잣

HERB
허브

basil	바질
mint	민트
dill	딜
oregano	오레가노
parsley	파슬리
thyme	타임
sage	세이지

SPICE
향신료

allspice	올스파이스 (자메이카 향신료)
caraway	캐러웨이
coriander	고수
fennel	펜넬 (회향)
garlic	마늘
ginger	생강
marjoram	마조람
nutmeg	육두구
pepper	후추
saffron	사프란
star anise	팔각
tarragon	타라곤
vanilla	바닐라

VEGETABLE
채소

carrot	당근
chili	고추
edamame	풋콩
sweet potato	고구마
tomato	토마토

GRAIN 곡물	
millet	수수
quinoa	퀴노아
sesame seed	참깨

OHTERS 기타	
butter	버터
buttermilk	버터밀크
caramel	캐러멜
cheddar cheese	체더 치즈
cotija cheese	코티하 치즈
feta cheese	페타 치즈
goat cheese	염소 치즈
manchego cheese	만체고 치즈
monterey jack cheese	몬터레이 잭 치즈
parmesan cheese	파르메산 치즈
swiss cheese	스위스 치즈
honey	꿀
maple syrup	메이플 시럽
milk	우유
mascarpone	마스카르포네
mushroom	버섯
oil	식용유
salt	소금
apple cider vinegar	사과 식초
champagne vinegar	샴페인 식초
red wine vinegar	레드와인 식초
white wine vinegar	화이트와인 식초
yogurt	요거트

CARAMEL 캐러멜

FRUIT
과일/열매

apple	사과
apricot	살구
banana	바나나
cherry	체리
lemon	레몬
lime	라임
mango	망고
passion fruit	패션프루트
peach	복숭아
pear	배
plum	자두
raisin	건포도

NUT
견과류

almond	아몬드
macadamia	마카다미아
peanut	땅콩
pecan	피칸

LIQUEUR / WINE
리큐르 / 와인

bourbon	버번 (위스키)
rum	럼

SPICE
향신료

cinnamon	시나몬
coffee	커피
nutmeg	육두구
vanilla	바닐라

VEGETABLE
채소

rhubarb	루바브

GRAIN
곡물

sesame seed	참깨

OHTERS
기타

chocolate (dark, milk, white)	초콜릿 (다크, 밀크, 화이트)
cream cheese	크림 치즈

 **COFFEE** 커피

FRUIT 과일/열매	
banana	바나나
cherry	체리
coconut	코코넛
date	대추
fig	무화과
lemon	레몬
lime	라임
orange	오렌지
pear	배
prune	건자두
raisin	건포도
mango	망고

LIQUEUR / WINE 리큐르 / 와인	
bourbon	버번 (위스키)
brandy	브랜디 (포도 발효 증류술)
cognac	코냑
rum	럼

NUT 견과류	
almond	아몬드
hazelnut	헤이즐넛
macadamia	마카다미아
pecan	피칸
walnut	호두

DARK CHOCOLATE 다크초콜릿

FRUIT 과일/열매	
apricot	살구
banana	바나나
cherry	체리
chestnut	밤
coconut	코코넛
currant	커런트
dates	대추
dried cherry	건체리
fig	무화과
gogi berry	구기자 열매
lemon	레몬
orange	오렌지
passion fruit	패션프루트
pear	배
prune	건자두
raisin	건포도
raspberry	라즈베리
strawberry	딸기

NUT 견과류	
almond	아몬드
brazilnut	브라질너트
cashewnut	캐슈넛
hazelnut	헤이즐넛
macadamia	마카다미아
peanut	땅콩
pecan	피칸
walnut	호두

LIQUEUR / WINE 리큐르 / 와인	
armagnac	아르마냑 (프랑스산 브랜디의 일종)
banyuls wine	바뉠스 와인 (강화 와인)
bourbon	버번 (위스키)
brandy	브랜디 (포도 발효 증류술)
cognac	코냑
port wine	포트 와인
rum	럼
sweet wine	스위트 와인

HERB
허브

basil	바질
lavender	라벤더
lemongrass	레몬그라스
mint	민트

SPICE
향신료

allspice	올스파이스 (자메이카 향신료)
anise	아니스
black pepper	흑후추
cardamom	카다멈
cinnamon	시나몬
clove	정향
coffee	커피
ginger	생강
nutmeg	육두구
vanilla	바닐라

GRAIN
곡물

oat	오트

OHTERS
기타

black tea	홍차
brown rice syrup	현미 시럽
butter	버터
butterscotch	버터스카치 (스카치 캔디)
caramel	캐러멜
cream cheese	크림 치즈
crème fraiche	크렘 프레슈
green tea	녹차
honey	꿀
maple syrup	메이플 시럽
milk	우유
mascarpone	마스카르포네
ricotta cheese	리코타 치즈
sour cream	사워 크림

MILK CHOCOLATE 밀크초콜릿

FRUIT 과일/열매	
apricot	살구
cherry	체리
chestnut	밤
coconut	코코넛
orange	오렌지
raspberry	라즈베리

SPICE 향신료	
cinnamon	시나몬
coffee	커피
ginger	생강

OHTERS 기타	
caramel	캐러멜
honey	꿀

NUT 견과류	
almond	아몬드
hazelnut	헤이즐넛
peanut	땅콩
pecan	피칸
walnut	호두

LIQUEUR / WINE 리큐르 / 와인	
rum	럼

HERB 허브	
lavender	라벤더

NOTE.

WHITE CHOCOLATE 화이트초콜릿

FRUIT
과일/열매

apricot	살구
banana	바나나
blackberry	블랙베리
blueberry	블루베리
cherry	체리
coconut	코코넛
concord grape	콩코드 포도 (미국의 포도)
cranberry	크랜베리
date	대추
fig	무화과
lemon	레몬
lime	라임
mango	망고
orange	오렌지
papaya	파파야
passion fruit	패션프루트
pear	배
persimmon	감
pomegranate	석류
prune	건자두
red currant	레드 커런트
strawberry	딸기

NUT
견과류

almond	아몬드
cashewnut	캐슈넛
hazelnut	헤이즐넛
macadamia	마카다미아
pistachio	피스타치오

HERB
허브

basil	바질
mint	민트

SPICE
향신료

allspice	올스파이스 (자메이카 향신료)
anise	아니스
cardamon	카다멈
cinnamon	시나몬
clove	정향
fennel	펜넬 (회향)
nutmeg	육두구
star anise	팔각
ginger	생강
tamarind	타마린드
vanilla	바닐라

LIQUEUR / WINE
리큐르 / 와인

rum	럼

VEGETABLE 채소	
rhubarb	루바브

OHTERS 기타	
caramel	캐러멜
cacao	카카오
honey	꿀
maple syrup	메이플 시럽
milk	우유
cream cheese	크림 치즈
cream	생크림
ricotta cheese	리코타 치즈
chocolate (dark, milk, white)	초콜릿 (다크, 밀크, 화이트)
oatmeal	오트밀

MAPLE SYRUP 메이플 시럽

FRUIT 과일/열매	
apple	사과
apricot	살구
banana	바나나
blueberry	블루베리
chestnut	밤
cranberry	크랜베리
fig	무화과
date	대추
lemon	레몬
lime	라임
orange	오렌지
peach	복숭아
pear	배
persimmon	감
pineapple	파인애플
plum	자두
prune	건자두
raisin	건포도
raspberry	라즈베리
quince	모과
strawberry	딸기

NUT 견과류	
almond	아몬드
cashewnut	캐슈넛
hazelnut	헤이즐넛
macadamia	마카다미아
pecan	피칸
pumpkin seed	호박씨
walnut	호두

LIQUEUR / WINE 리큐르 / 와인	
bourbon	버번 (위스키)
rum	럼

SPICE 향신료	
cardamom	카다멈
cinnamon	시나몬
clove	정향
coffee	커피
ginger	생강
nutmeg	육두구

VEGETABLE 채소	
carrot	당근
rhubarb	루바브
sweet potato	고구마

GRAIN 곡물	
corn	옥수수
corn meal	옥수수가루
oat	오트
rice	쌀

OHTERS 기타	
buttermilk	버터밀크
caramel	캐러멜
chocolate (dark, milk, white)	초콜릿 (다크, 밀크, 화이트)
cream cheese	크림 치즈
granola	그래놀라
miso	미소 (일본식 된장)

VANILLA 바닐라

FRUIT 과일/열매	
apple	사과
apricot	살구
banana	바나나
cherry	체리
coconut	코코넛
fig	무화과
lemon	레몬
melon	멜론
orange	오렌지
peach	복숭아
pear	배
plum	자두
raspberry	라즈베리
strawberry	딸기

NUT 견과류	
almond	아몬드
cashewnut	캐슈넛

LIQUEUR / WINE 리큐르 / 와인	
brandy	브랜디 (포도 발효 증류술)
wine	와인
vodka	보드카

HERB 허브	
basil	바질
lavender	라벤더
rosemary	로즈마리
mint	민트
thyme	타임

SPICE 향신료	
black pepper	흑후추
cardamom	카다멈
cinnamon	시나몬
clove	정향
coffee	커피
ginger	생강
nutmeg	육두구
saffron	사프란

VEGETABLE 채소	
beet	비트
chili	고추
pumpkin	호박
rhubarb	루바브
tomato	토마토

GRAIN 곡물	
green bean	깍지콩
oat	오트

OHTERS 기타	
caramel	캐러멜
dark chocolate	다크초콜릿
maple syrup	메이플 시럽
tea	차
yogurt	요거트

YOGURT 요거트

FRUIT 과일/열매	
apple	사과
apricot	살구
avocado	아보카도
banana	바나나
blackberry	블랙베리
blueberry	블루베리
cherry	체리
coconut	코코넛
fig	무화과
lemon	레몬
lime	라임
mango	망고
nectarine	천도복숭아
orange	오렌지
papaya	파파야
peach	복숭아
pineapple	파인애플
raisin	건포도
raspberry	라즈베리
strawberry	딸기

NUT 견과류	
hazelnut	헤이즐넛
pecan	피칸
pistachio	피스타치오
walnut	호두

HERB 허브	
basil	바질
chervil	처빌
dill	딜
mint	민트
oregano	오레가노
thyme	타임

SPICE 향신료	
cinnamon	시나몬
coriander	고수
fennel	펜넬 (회향)
garlic	마늘
tamarind	타마린드
vanilla	바닐라

VEGETABLE
채소

arugula	루콜라
beet	비트
carrot	당근
paprika	파프리카
rhubarb	루바브
spinach	시금치
tomato	토마토
watercress	물냉이

OHTERS
기타

balsamic vinegar	발사믹 식초
feta cheese	페타 치즈
goat cheese	염소 치즈
mushroom	버섯
olive oil	올리브오일
red wine vinegar	레드와인 식초
sherry vinegar	셰리주 식초

GRAIN
곡물

barley	보리
chickpea	병아리콩
fava bean	누에콩
lentil	렌틸콩
lima bean	리마콩
oat	오트
rice	쌀
quinoa	퀴노아
white bean	흰 강낭콩

HONEY 꿀

FRUIT 과일/열매	
apple	사과
apricot	살구
banana	바나나
chestnut	밤
coconut	코코넛
date	대추
fig	무화과
grape	포도
grapefruit	자몽
guava	구아바
honeydew melon	허니듀 멜론
kumquat	금귤
lemon	레몬
lime	라임
lychee	리치
melon	멜론
nectarine	천도복숭아
orange	오렌지
papaya	파파야
peach	복숭아
pear	배
persimmon	감
pineapple	파인애플
plantain	플랜테인 (바나나의 일종)
plum	자두
pomegranate	석류

prune	건자두
quince	모과
raspberry	라즈베리
raisin	건포도
red currant	레드 커런트

NUT 견과류	
pecan	피칸
pinenut	잣
pistachio	피스타치오
sunflower seed	해바라기씨
walnut	호두

LIQUEUR / WINE 리큐르 / 와인	
cognac	코냑

HERB 허브	
lavender	라벤더
rosemary	로즈마리

SPICE
향신료

cardamom	카다멈
clove	정향
cinnamon	시나몬
coffee	커피
ginger	생강
mustard	겨자
nutmeg	육두구
black pepper	흑후추
tarragon	타라곤
vanilla	바닐라

VEGETABLE
채소

beet	비트
carrot	당근
chili	고추
pumpkin	호박
yam	마

GRAIN
곡물

lentil	렌틸콩
pumpkin seed	호박씨
sesame seed	참깨
quinoa	퀴노아

OHTERS
기타

brown sugar	황설탕
chocolate (dark, milk, white)	초콜릿 (다크, 밀크, 화이트)
buttermilk	버터밀크
cheese	치즈
blue cheese	블루 치즈
cream cheese	크림 치즈
pecorino cheese	페코리노 치즈
ricotta cheese	리코타 치즈
goat cheese	양젖 치즈
mascarpone	마스카르포네
miso	미소 (일본식 된장)
granola	그래놀라
oatmeal	오트밀
balsamic vinegar	발사믹 식초
yogurt	요거트

PATISSERIE ERIC

DESSERT PAIRING BOOK

초판 1쇄 인쇄   2024년 05월 01일

초판 1쇄 발행   2024년 05월 17일

지은이 김동석 | **영문 번역** Kim Eunice | **펴낸이** 박윤선 | **발행처** (주)더테이블

기획·편집 박윤선 | **교정** 김영란 | **디자인** 김보라 | **영업·마케팅** 김남권, 조용훈, 문성빈 | **경영지원** 김효선, 이정민

주소 경기도 부천시 조마루로385번길 122 삼보테크노타워 2002호

홈페이지 www.icoxpublish.com | **쇼핑몰** www.baek2.kr (백두도서쇼핑몰) | **인스타그램** @thetable_book

이메일 thetable_book@naver.com | **전화** 032) 674-5685 | **팩스** 032) 676-5685

등록 2022년 8월 4일 제 386-2022-000050 호 | **ISBN** 979-11-92855-11-0 (14590), 979-11-92855-09-7 (14590) [세트]

First edition printed   May 1, 2024

First edition published   May 17, 2024

Author Kim Dongseok | **Translated by** Kim Eunice | **Publisher** Bak Yunseon | **Published by** THETABLE Inc.

Plan & Edit Bak Yunseon | **Proofreading** Kim Youngran | **Design** Kim Bora

Sales/Marketing Kim Namkwon, Cho Yonghoon, Moon Seongbin | **Management support** Kim Hyoseon, Lee Jungmin

Address 122, Jomaru-ro 385beon-gil, Bucheon-si, Gyeonggi-do, Republic of Korea

Website www.icoxpublish.com | **Instagram** @thetable_book

E-mail thetable_book@naver.com | **Phone** 82-32-674-5685

Registration date August 4, 2022 | **Registration number** 386-2022-000050

ISBN 979-11-92855-11-0 (14590), 979-11-92855-09-7 (14590) [SET]